Gift

From Spiritual Wealth
To Financial Wealth

Elizabeth Francis

www.capallbann.co.uk

Gift
From Spiritual Wealth
To Financial Wealth

©Copyright 2011 Elizabeth Francis

ISBN 186163 322 X
ISBN 13   9781861633224

Cover design by Elizabeth Francis
Cover layout by HR Design

Published by:

Capall Bann Publishing
Auton Farm
Milverton
Somerset
TA4 1NE

Dedicated to my family, especially my daughter, friends, clients and all those who have crossed my path.

Co-edited by Macdara Ó hUallacháin Graham

Elizabeth Francis

Formerly working in the oil, gas and defence industries, in the early nineties Elizabeth achieved a complete turn-around to become an internationally recognised spiritual service provider. For almost twenty years, Elizabeth has used her gifts as a Light-worker to operate within the realms of channeling, mediumship, clairvoyance, clairaudience and clairsentience; she is a past and future lives seer, a shaman, a remote viewer, and a spell crafter and caster.

Elizabeth is a qualified complementary health therapist with qualifications in counselling, anatomy and physiology. She is a Consultant Member of Russell Grant's BAPS and a member of the Affiliation of Crystal & Gem Therapists, the World Federation of Healer and the Spiritual Workers Association.

Elizabeth has appeared on the Steve Nolan Show, in the Spirit Trap - A Ghost Story documentary and was invited by Crusader Films to join a team producing a documentary about the hauntings in Pembroke Castle. She has also been published in magazines, including Spiritual Lifestyles and the World Federation of Healers member's magazine.

Her website address is: www.elizabethfrancis.co.uk

Contents

Introduction   1
1. Working With Spirit   3
2. The Nature of Spirit   10
3. Spiritual Wealth   15
4. You are a Psychic   19
5. How Do I Prove To Myself I Am Psychic?   31
6. Interpreting Spiritual Messages   39
7. Keep Your Feet on the Ground   46
8. Entering the World of Metaphysics, Cosmology and Cosmogony   56
9. The Importance of Thought   63
10. The Role of the Light-being   66
11. Where Does Religion Fit Into All this?   73
12. Contacting Spirit   75
13. Blindsides, Self-empowerment and Self-discipline   79
14. Commitment to Spirit   85
15. The Path of the Practising Psychic   88
16. Seven Rites of Passage of a Psychic   94
17. Spiritual Journeys Can't Be Rushed?   102
18. "Spirit Helps Those Who Help Themselves"   107
19. Walk Your Talk as a Practising Psychic   110
20. Dreams, Correspondences, Symbolism, Signs, Elements, the Elementals and Divination   118
21. Tools of the Trade   128
22. Unlocking the door of Knowledge   135
23. Experience is the Ultimate Teacher   139
24. Technique and Structure   147
25. How to Divine   153
26. Turning Professional   191
27. The Chapter Not To Skip - Business Sense   194
28. Finding Work - Agency vs. Independent   201
29. Being a Professional Psychic   207
Appendix 1 Elizabeth Francis Keywords for Tarot   216
Appendix 2   224
Appendix 3   228

Introduction

There are many ways in which a person can turn his or her spiritual wealth into financial wealth, and the method outlined here in Gift is just one of them.

Gift has been written to provide insight and direction to walking the path of a practising and professional psychic. It takes you on a thought provoking and sometimes challenging journey.

As the journey is also one of self-discovery, Gift begins with the concept of Spirit and it's purpose. It also explains how to identify the myriad of physical reactions that can be experienced when Spirit is present.

This book has been written bearing in mind that above all else free will and self-responsibility are sacrosanct.

1. Working With Spirit

There's an age-old saying, "Spirit works in mysterious ways" and no truer words have ever been spoken: Spirit is of the Divine and is timeless. It is both elusive and invisible to most of us - and when it does make itself known, it does so in very subtle ways. Well, most of the time.

It may not be easy for some to accept or understand, but we all possess a natural ability to work with Spirit. Whether we realise it or not we all use the ability in one way or another throughout our lives. It is called intuition, a gut feeling or a hunch. Some follow their intuition blindly, others ignore it and then there are those who are drawn to harness and use it as a tool to help them live their lives.

It is a very sweeping statement to claim that we all work with Spirit unless you take into account the mindset of reincarnation. From that perspective we do nothing but interact with Spirit.

Reincarnation

Transmigration of the soul is a mindset based upon the belief that we return to the earth plane after we die, and do so as many times as is necessary until we have perfected the human condition. To achieve this we reincarnate.

Therefore, we exist not only as human beings - that of the self, the finite which inhabits the earth plane, but also our Higher-selves, that of Spirit and our Light-being state, the infinite which resides within all the planes of existence.

The number of planes of existence is dependent upon the different mindsets. For this purpose, seven planes are being used, which are as follows:

Table I	
The Seven Planes of Existence	
The First	The Etheric
The Second	The Emotional
The Third	The Mental
The Fourth	The Astral
The Fifth	The Etheric Template
The Sixth	The Celestial
The Seventh	The Causal or Ketheric

The etheric, the first plane of existence, is a semi-physical plane and the state before manifestation of the physical plane. It is in our Light-being states that we choose and plan each lifetime before we reincarnate and our Higher-self and self, which has a collection of selves within it, enact those plans.

Although incarnation causes a change in our relationship with Spirit at the time of conception we are never separated from Spirit, therefore we are all psychic. This means we have the ability to see Spirit's work from the moment of our conception and throughout our lives.

As babies and children we are able to converse with Spirit as a matter of course, and parents often witness this. By the time we are twenty-one, many of us have forgotten how to converse with Spirit as we did when young. Others have not.

The resurfacing of those memories can occur at any given moment throughout our lives. As they do, our instincts become stronger until they cannot be ignored. This resurrection usually occurs when we need Spirit the most, but it can also happen as a matter of course. Whether we realise this at the time is another issue.

How We Function

A prerequisite to working with Spirit is to have a good sense of humour, the source of which is yourself. Humour is one of the greatest gifts we are given. It literally lifts the spirits and by doing so can remove the barriers that stop us appreciating how we function.

We function through our five senses, so it is through our five senses that we interact with Spirit. This interaction can affect us mentally, emotionally and physically. The purpose of interacting with Spirit is for us to receive information - directly or indirectly. This information can assist us to live our lives and working with it develops our sixth sense – intuition.

Working with intuition on a conscious level enables life to be viewed from two perspectives, the 'Little Picture' and the 'Big Picture'.

This is where it helps to have a sense of humour: from 'Little Picture', it often appears that there is no rhyme or reason for certain events. The 'Big Picture' makes the rhymes and provides the reasons by taking into account the concepts of reincarnation and that we all choose our lives before we are born. It provides the missing links that enable us to trace the continual input of Spirit in our lives so we can attain enlightenment, if we so choose.

The Light of Life

Our Higher-self, which serves as the intermediary between our self and Light-being States, holds all the information we need to know about our selves. It knows what it is doing and understands how to work with us, because we are a part of it.

It's the self in its human condition, which stumbles around in the dark and hurts itself as it trips over the seemingly never-ending metaphorical coffee tables of life.

Our Higher-selves offer us a never-ending supply of lit candles to illuminate our paths. These candles are the helping hands of Spirit and can take the form of people, thoughts, visions or events, whether they are major or minor. Irrespective of the form this help takes or how it appears, it is up to us whether to accept the helping hand, or not.

If we accept, it is because we used our psychic ability to identify the help being offered. Again, it is then it is up to us to take responsibility for using that help wisely. Unless we take full responsibility for the choices we make, we cannot work with Spirit in a meaningful and productive way. By doing so, what is revealed to us is our enlightened state.

Enlightenment

Our Higher-selves acts as a guide through our individual journeys to enlightenment.

We all experience enlightenment many times during our lives. Some of you may have already gone through enlightenment, others will have and not realised it.

Enlightenment takes place when our Higher-selves contact our Light-being States, and this process enables us to function as Light-workers. We will go into greater detail about this concept later in the book, but for now a quick definition of a Light-worker: A person who consciously works so they can become the best of who they are in their human state.

But how can we achieve this? It would appear that we're pre-disposed to it. Although we are members of the animal kingdom, there are several key differences that separate us from the other species. It is thought that these differences are due to forty-nine segments of the human genome, human accelerated regions[1] (HARs) 1 – 49. Har-1 takes us away from the evolutionary path and into the murky waters of interventionists.

Therefore, we are not enslaved by working instinctively at one with Mother Nature as other creatures are. Instead, from

1. Katherine Pollard: What Makes Us Human

very early on, our ancestors developed an innate relationship with Mother Nature, which was built upon our animal instincts.

One of the results of this was to create a need for something bigger and better than ourselves and then idolise it. This desire is what makes us human. It could be said that Mother Nature is the first archetype of the all seeing, all knowing Spirit.

The plethora of philosophies and religions that exist today is testament to this powerful spiritual aspect - the Light-being State that we have within. This power can be detrimental or beneficial depending upon who we are. Who we are is dependant upon our own decision-making.

Working with Spirit as a Psychic

Many of us come to a time in our lives when we have a need to nurture, develop and express our spiritual selves. Since we are all unique, our concept of Spirit is wide, varied and continually evolving.

For that reason there are many paths that can be walked, sometimes simultaneously, to achieve the same goal. No one path is better than another; it is how it's walked that is the determining factor. By recognising our intuitive abilities as a gift, we walk the path of the psychic.

Although we are all psychic, there are different categories of psychic: those who do not practice, practicing psychics and those who turn professional. Practicing and professional psychics work with Spirit on a conscious level. They receive, process and deliver information from Spirit. Professional psychics turn this process into a service and receive payment.

The word 'psychic' can mean different things to different people and the reaction to the word will be according to personal experiences - even if the experience is no experience. It's an umbrella word used to describe something largely unknown to us: the Workings of Spirit (WoS).

For simplicity's sake, when I use the word 'psychic', I refer to the 'umbrella' concept. Clarification regarding the different definitions is given later in this book.

Psychic ability stems from the original practices of shamanism - the first practical religion and as such secured the existence of the human race. Shamanism developed from our relationship with Mother Nature.

Over the millennia this ancient practice evolved into the concept of spirituality, which in turn gave birth to a variety of religions. In time the science of psychology was developed from that parapsychology, which investigates psychic phenomena.

The majority of the WoS takes place in the higher planes of existence where our Higher-selves function. The astral plane is a bridge that the High-self uses to communicate with the self, which resides the lower levels of existence.

So from the human perspective, we consciously pick up on the WoS within the etherics. This means that the WoS are at their most obvious in our pre-sub-conscious, the state below the sub-conscious state, where the mental and emotional planes of existence cannot be reported.

By the time they reach our conscious states the WoS are invisible to us unless we use our psychic abilities to contact Spirit.

There are an infinite number of ways that we are able to contact and work with Spirit. The more open we are to the ways of WoS the broader the spectrum of activity and abilities will be.

One of the ways these workings make themselves known is through thought. For example, when the solution to a problem strikes us out of the blue, the 'eureka moment', the light bulb turning on above a person's head is a very apt description of the WoS.

The purpose of developing our psychic abilities is to be able to see, hear and/or feel WoS within, on a conscious level. Being privy to such workings influences our decision-making and therefore our actions.

There are no given parameters when working with Spirit, so the only guideline is this: to respect Spirit by working in a moral and ethical manner. An appropriate analogy is that most of us would not consider using another's belongings without asking permission first and saying thank you afterward. Likewise when interacting with Spirit. Respect Spirit and you respect yourself. Respect yourself and you can encounter the nature of Spirit as you walk your path.

2. The Nature of Spirit

How Spirit works no one really knows because the nature of Spirit is held within silence, is elusive, it is the unknown, that which is hidden and beyond our understanding. What we do know is that Spirit resides within us and touches us in a myriad of mysterious ways.

An upshot of this concept means Spirit is automatically instilled in the mind of all life forms, the purpose of which is to house the soul as it undertakes a journey of a lifetime.

The soul is the consciousness of conscience - that vital principle that makes us compassionate beings and as such we become the embodiment of Spirit itself within our human state. Without the soul, Spirit cannot live within us and we cannot be a part of it.

The soul being the seat of life in our human state enables us to access our Higher-selves on a conscious level. This in turn enables us to interact with Spirit. The information received is a result of this interaction and is held by our sixth sense, which enables our psychic abilities to emerge.

This emergence enables us as human beings to connect to our Light-being State via our Higher-selves. Once this link is established we can function as Light-workers in our human state. Thus the nature of Spirit can be revealed.

Look around as well as within and you will find that the nature of Spirit comes in many guises, they are all relevant and the choice is yours. One of them is the established religions and mindsets such as the Shinto Kojiki, the Hindu Vedas, the Bible, the Torah, the Koran and Buddhist texts.

Turn your eyes to the not so well known belief systems such as the Gnostics and Druidism, as well as the gospels that cannot be found in the Bible, such as the gospels according to Mary Magdalene and Thomas.

The practice of bibliomancy is also valuable when seeking the nature of Spirit. Opening a book at any page and reading whatever sentence your eyes fall upon can give you guidance from Spirit that cannot be gained by any other method.

Spirit uses our individual uniqueness to make itself known to us. Therefore your interpretation will be very different to that of another. By recognising your own interpretation, rather than following another's, you will be allowing yourself to develop your theories as to the nature of Spirit.

Your concept of this subject may be very different and therefore you may find what you have just read challenging. That reaction is very positive because it can indicate that you have an open mind.

Not having any preconceived ideas about the nature of Spirit is also a very positive sign, because often established ideas can stop people from recognising the vastness and magnificence of it all.

Working with a concept that you feel most comfortable with enables you to be true to yourself. This doesn't mean that over time your concept should or should not change, that isn't the point. The point is you cannot evolve unless you are true to yourself and remain so, despite what others may think or say.

Dismissing a concept because it doesn't 'fit in' with the 'norm' is one of the major reasons why people do not follow their spiritual paths.

Once you start your journey of self-discovery then you will find like-minded people. This is when you come across the concept of the Collective, another aspect of the nature of Spirit.

The Collective Consciousness

The Collective is a concept based on the premise that all our individual Higher-selves work toward the same goal, there is no division on the higher levels and thus the Collective Consciousness is produced. The goal of the Collective is 'the betterment', whether it is the betterment of the human being or another existence.

This concept is not necessarily affiliated with any religion or organisation but there are many religions and organizations that use it.

The Higher-self is based upon belief in the self not the viewpoint of others. It places behaviour above ambition and by doing so allows cooperation to develop. With cooperation comes peace and harmony.

The concept of the Collective is an ancient one that has been reinvented with each new generation. It is this continual reinvention that enables us, and it, to evolve spiritually, emotionally, physically and mentally.

On the higher levels the Collective works in unison with itself and our Higher-selves are a part of that process. Our physical selves aspire to work in unison with others since we are tribal by nature. Our uniqueness as individuals demands that we stand alone, and our self-empowerment enables us to do so.

As a result, some people find themselves becoming isolationists by default as they start to work with their Higher-selves on a conscious level. By doing so they are discovering their individualism whilst identifying their role within the Collective.

Isolationism

Isolationism is an integral part of understanding the Collective Consciousness and what can counter-balance it are our natural instincts to be a part of a tribe.

From the spiritual perspective, the more a person develops his or her psychic abilities the further he or she is pushing themselves away from their kinship and the more they become isolated.

Finding your environment is becoming intolerable identifies isolationism knocking on your door. The intolerance comes from feeling that you have nothing in common with many who make up your social circle. If this occurs you are in the process of leaving, or have left, your tribe.

Until you find a replacement tribe you are an isolationist but on the higher levels you are still an active and integral part of the Collective. That never changes, despite what we do on the Earth plane.

Although it is not easy to come out of a tribe, it is more than made up for when you find a new tribe where you are accepted.

Newton's Laws of Motion and the Isolationist

As moving from one tribe to another isn't avoidable, a way of softening the process is to apply the third Law of Motion: to every action there is an equal and opposite reaction. Therefore, if we do not act, we cannot change our circumstances. If we act we can change our circumstances.

Therefore, if we do not act, we cannot change our circumstances. If we act we can change our circumstances.

Our survival instincts come to the fore when the urge to act and leave one tribe becomes a force that cannot be ignored. Our survival instincts demand we put ourselves first, unless we are a parent with young children.

Putting oneself first is not being selfish, as many think. It is being a realist. How can anyone create a balanced and healthy lifestyle if they are living in an environment that prevents them from becoming who they are? No one can. And no reasonable person would expect anyone to. So the question isn't whether to leave a tribe when circumstances demand it, but how.

A way forward through what some may consider being the isolationist's paradox is to recognize the importance of balance - the Golden Mean - the Principle of Polarity. Balance is based upon everything having an equal opposite. Employing balance can be a solution. Balance in this instant can be to acknowledge that moving from one tribe to another may be an ongoing process throughout spiritual evolvement.

From a personal perspective that means the tribe you are being drawn to may not be the tribe you end up with. You may end up with the tribe you presently find intolerable. So when you do leave, do so in stages, preparing for the way ahead and choosing carefully the bridges you wish to burn, if any, as you go.

Balance

The areas that will enable you to achieve balance can be found in two of the human traits, which are selfishness and self-sacrifice. Focus on the role they have to play when turning your spiritual wealth into financial wealth whilst answering these questions:

• Is it selfish to put yourself first and if by doing so, are you taking responsibility for your own actions?

• Is it selfish if you take what isn't yours or claim something at someone else's expense, especially when on closer inspection you don't actually need it?

• Does it help if you are self-sacrificing out of habit and therefore as a matter of course?

These questions can be used as guidelines and the answers may appear obvious, but think again more carefully since there are no definitive answers. And they are entirely subjective to circumstance.

Bear in mind that it is the nature of Spirit within us that enables our individualism to form the Collective Consciousness which itself falls outside of both culture and creed.

3. Spiritual Wealth

Spiritual wealth lies within. It cannot be bought, borrowed or stolen. It is up to the individual concerned as to whether or not they wish to embrace this type of resource.

In order to embrace it, there needs to be an awareness of the nature of Spirit. If you are of the opinion that there is something more out there that is beyond explanation, then you are aware of the nature of Spirit. An awareness of Spirit is having an acceptance of self.

As to its function, although subjective, the existence of Spirit is the reason why you are drawn to contact it in the first place.

The most common ways of contacting Spirit are through prayer and/or talking to oneself. Once contact with Spirit is made it is possible to start the process of witnessing the nature of Spirit and how it works. When the WoS are witnessed, we can then start to understand that it is the nature of Spirit that lies within each one of us that is the true gift.

Finding the Gift

We are all born with the gift of an abundance of spiritual wealth, some of which comes in the form of psychic gifts. When identified as such, these gifts develop into abilities, which when harnessed and used, become skills.

The only thing that stops us from working with and benefiting from these psychic gifts is our self-doubt.

We step onto the path of the psychic when we stop doubting ourselves. As a consequence we automatically start to work with our Higher-selves on a conscious level.

Having a conscious awareness of the WoS and/or a belief in

Spirit isn't a fundamental requirement to experiencing psychic phenomena – which is when Spirit contacts us directly.

A conscious awareness of the WoS and/or belief in and commitment to Spirit is necessary if we wish to develop our psychic abilities into skills. Therefore the decision to commit has to be based upon Free Will.

Free Will is sacrosanct and it is paramount that everyone exercises this precious gift on a conscious level. Only with conscious commitment to Spirit can we turn our spiritual wealth into financial wealth. By consciously committing to Spirit we are committing to ourselves.

It doesn't matter what form Spirit takes at the time of commitment, the choice is up to the individual, who is always free to convert from one form to another throughout the length of his or her spiritual journey.

Spiritual Wealth and Metaphysics

The word metaphysics is made up of two Greek words, meta – beyond, and physics – of the physical world. Metaphysics is the philosophical study of being and knowing, the nature of reality and the intangible. It is based on the concept that the cosmos and everything in it has been produced by vibration and the effect these vibrations have had on the ethers.

The complexity of being a practising psychic reflects both the complexities of life and the variety of spiritual paths. There are the universally culturally accepted paths that lead to Spirit, while others remain elusive and hidden. Metaphysics is one of those other paths.

The Laws of Metaphysics are based on theoretical principles that have evolved over thousands of years. It started with shamanism, continued with the emergence of philosophy and some religions before last – but not least – these ideas gave birth to magik (sic) and alchemy, the forerunners of the sciences of today. Its greatest strength is that metaphysics attempts to provide answers to that which science cannot. The main questions are "why are we here?" and "what are we here for?"

We know that Spirit is usually invisible, often elusive and comes in all shapes and sizes. This combination leads to the concept that when working with Spirit, anything can happen and all things are possible.

Metaphysics embraces Spirit by allowing us to entertain the belief that not only does Spirit exist, but that it can also portray a multitude of existences. Therefore the concept of Spirit is not only to be associated with those who have died. It also includes Angels, ETs., (extra terrestrials) and the elementals.

With the advent of quantum mechanics and physics it is becoming widely accepted that life in all its forms has a spiritual counterpart. Furthermore, this spiritual counterpart survives before, during and after the life.

Therefore, from a human standpoint, metaphysics enables Spirit to be a place where we are before we are born, return after we have died, and are whilst they are functioning within the human condition.

The concept of Spirit is important as it contains all known and unknown knowledge concerning cosmos. The cosmos is made up all known and unknown life. This includes universe, multi-verses and parallel existences, which include before time began, as well as until the end of time - all of which provide us a true likeness to Spirit

Although metaphysics embraces Spirit's existence, there is no proof that Spirit does exist and that is why it is a belief. We all need something to believe in, even if it is the belief that Spirit doesn't exist.

From Spiritual Wealth to Financial Wealth

The belief in Spirit enables the wealth of it to take many forms. The obvious riches are mental, spiritual, emotional, physical and, since we live in a material world, material wellbeing.

Spirit knows no boundaries or restrictions. So by definition, the same applies to spiritual wealth. Since Spirit is whatever you perceive it to be and more, so too is spiritual wealth.

Therefore, it is up to you to develop your image of Spirit and identify your source of spiritual wealth. No one can do that for you, so please do not look to another in the hope that they can.

Spiritual gifts can formulate financial wealth. Financial wealth does not reflect the true wealth gained from working with Spirit, it is simply a by-product. The most precious form of spiritual wealth surely has to be Divine Intervention - where Spirit intervenes to save us from ourselves.

4. You are a Psychic

Recognizing that you are a psychic is the first step. Believing that you are psychic is the second step. Developing and using your psychic abilities is a massive leap of faith in yourself and therefore showing that you have faith in Spirit.

A lot of people are perfectly willing to accept that others are psychic but find it difficult to accept that they themselves are. This is despite the fact that many have undergone psychic phenomena or been told by a professional that they are psychically active.

Personal disbelief in psychic ability is perfectly understandable since metaphysics isn't included in the school curriculum. The medical profession will often diagnose such experiences as symptoms of a malfunction of the brain or a person suffering from delusions.

There is no doubt that some medical conditions have similar symptoms, but the vast majority of people that experience such 'symptoms' may well be experiencing psychic phenomena. Furthermore, the medical profession itself is backed up by some less enlightened individuals within the various religious fraternities who view such abilities as a threat to their very existence.

Whether the powers that be like it or not, if you see, feel and/or hear Spirit you are psychic. Table II, below, shows all the psychic medium terms and definitions available at the time of printing. When reading through it, tick the definitions you may think or know you have experienced, even if it is only once. Use this table as a checklist of how you are developing.

| Table II |
| Psychic Terms and Definitions |

√	Term	Meaning	Definition
	Clairvoyance	Clear seeing	Seeing spirits as though they were in their physical bodies. Visualization Pictures in the mind's eye.
		Peripheral	Flashes, shadows, movement out of the corner of the eye.
	Clairaudience (Spirit wish to communicate)	Clear hearing	Hearing voices or sounds of any type, including tinnitus.
	Clairsentience	Clear sensing, touching & being touched	Feeling the ailment or emotional state of a person when alive or at the time of dying.
	Clairalience	Clear smelling	Smelling Spirit, e.g. cigarette smoke, perfume etc.
	Clairgustance	Clear tasting	Tasting Spirit food or taste derived from an ailment or after death.
	Claircognizance	Clear knowing	Receiving knowledge without learning it.
	Mediumship	Telepathic agents	Communicates with Spirit.

	Telekinetic	automatic handwriting, the voice moving objects with the mind.
Mediumship II		
Precognitive	Future sight	Information regarding the future that cannot be deduced from circumstances unfolding in the present.

Below are some examples of how Spirit makes itself known to us through our physical bodies. You will see that the nervous system seems to be the favourite source of contact.

- Itching may not be the onset of hives or insect bites. It can also be Spirit touching you.
- Shivers or a temperature drop isn't necessarily the onset of a cold; it could be Spirit moving through you.
- A sudden rise in body temperature is often associated with hot flushes and the onset of menopause. This is also associated with Spirit working within you, since the older women get the more powerful they become. Men also experience this sensation.
- Seeing flashes of light, shadows, indescribable movement of some form out of the corner of your eye, which is often associated with peripheral vision problems, can be Spirit trying to make itself known to you through your peripheral vision.

Obviously, if you experience one or more of the above symptoms continuously, or they become uncomfortably intrusive, common sense demands you go to the doctor and get checked out. Such experiences denote you have activated your psychic abilities and are in contact with Spirit.

21

This activation enables your psychic 'memory', which includes memories of your past lives, to surface. During this process all the knowledge you hold within from your previous reincarnations becomes available to you in this lifetime.

At this stage most people are totally unaware that the process has started. Some may have begun to suspect if not think, "something is going on" beyond their present understanding but it is so elusive most people keep quiet about what they may or may not be experiencing.

These moments can be quite disconcerting and some think they are actually 'going mad'. Again, this is understandable when you consider you may be:

• Seeing something that is not there.
• Responding to a voice when no one has spoken (talking to yourself).
• Turning around to find no one is there when you where sure there was.
• Experiencing disassociated thoughts coming through and wondering why.

All of these incidents are signs that you are conversant with Spirit at a level that is affecting you physically.

Try not to allow your lack of knowledge within this field to cause you to dismiss the fact that you are psychic. If you were not psychic you could not have encountered such experiences. Table III opposite denotes a list of psychic abilities and their definitions:

Acknowledging You Are Psychic

Acknowledgement is based upon the acceptance you that are a psychic. Acceptance is necessary if you wish to benefit from your gifts. It is not easy to accept that you are psychic when you haven't been brought up in an environment that encourages open mindedness and freedom of choice.

The favourite response from someone who has been

Table III Skills Derived from Psychic Abilities	
Glossolalia	Gift of Tongues, unintelligible language.
Telepathy	Transference of information from one mind source to another.
ESP Extra Sensory Perception	The acquisition of information.
Precognitive	To view or know the future.
Psychokinesis	To move matter with the mind.
Automatic Handwriting	To write messages received from Spirit without conscious thought or interference from self.
Cryptomnesia	Linked to Past-life memories.
Scrying	Crystal ball or water/black ink reading.
Psychometry	Reading objects.
Déjà vu	Current events being experienced before or reenacting the future.
Astral Projection	The ability to leave the physical body and become active on the astral planes within the etherics.
Psychic Artists	The ability to draw people's guides, angels and deceased loved ones.
Mediumship	The ability to converse with those in Spirit.

advised they are psychically active - but are never the less still skeptical, is "If I were psychic why couldn't I have seen what was going to happen?"

And that is a very good question. The answer to this is three-fold, the first being that we are often too close to our own situation to be able to see it clearly. Secondly, you cannot assume that a person who is psychic can gain insight on demand without the necessary understanding of the experience. Finally, it is only when a person takes note of their instincts that they can have the ability to 'see' what will occur.

Such misconceptions show that people expect too much of themselves and therefore of Spirit.

It takes just as much skill, technique and discipline for a psychic to do an accurate reading for his or her self as it does to read for another person. It isn't that people should not read for themselves, as some believe, it is because they haven't learned how too.

Learning how to can only be achieved by acknowledging and accepting that you are psychic. Then you can learn to distance yourself from your situation and by doing so read for yourself.

Let's Get Physical

Although I have no medical training, I have spent years investigating the connection between the functions of our body and its reaction to psychic phenomena. I work from the premise that all matter is a collection of vibrating particles and there are no clear demarcations between the different parts of the body.

My work focuses mainly upon the brain - an electro-chemical organ - and its function. A summary of my findings to date is shown in Table IV

Table IV		
Sensory and Cognitive Correspondences		
Part of the Brain	Physical Function	Psychic Function
Auditory System	Hearing	Clairaudience
Central Nervous and Endocrine Systems	The Mind	Claircognizance (Knowing)
Digestive System	Taste	Clairgustance
Main Olfactory System	Smell	Clairalience
Somatosensory System	Touch	Clairsentience
Visual System	Sight	Clairvoyance

Let's Get Mechanical

Our bodies have been tailored to meet how our psychic abilities work within the planes of existence. By this I mean that the human body is a marvel of engineering, but only because its etheric template enables it to be so.

Without the electro-chemical workings of the brain our psychic abilities could not exist in the format that they do. Therefore it really does help to have a basic understanding of the correlation between how the brain works and psychic ability.

Clairaudience (Hearing) is when a person is able to hear the sounds produced by Spirit. On the earth plane sound is produced by disturbances that cause vibrations. The vibrations produce sound waves, which bounce off matter. Sound is the result.

Although all matter vibrates, the matter that supports sound (air, gases, water, wood, steel etc) is called a medium. The medium dictates the speed sound travels. Sound is measured in decibels (dB). Each decibel is one tenth of a bel. Basically it works like this, the greater the disturbance, the louder the sound. The number of vibrations or cycles per second makes up the frequency, which also determines the pitch of sound.

The range of audible frequencies we hear is determined by age. Young people with no hearing challenges hear within a range of 20 to 20,000 Hz per second. As we get older (or if we are exposed to long periods of loud noise over a period of time), the higher frequencies are lost.

Different species have different ranges of hearing, the range humans function within is referred to as sonic, or audio. The ranges that we are unable to hear are known as Infrasound and Ultrasound. Infrasound is produced from a low number of vibrations per second. Ultrasound is produced from the higher number of vibrations per second. Wildlife communicates on these levels.

Those who hear voices and/or sounds that others cannot are using their auditory system to access the sounds made within the planes of existence. People with clairaudient skills have broken through the physical barrier produced by their auditory system.

This breakthrough also includes the infra- and ultrasound levels used by animals and plants, and thus such individuals can hold conversations with all plant and animal life. As a result, their auditory system has connected to the hyper-communication network.[2]

Put in layman terms, hyper-communication is an invisible communications network produced by our DNA, which in a sense acts as both a transmitter and receiver of information.

---

2 Hyper-communicaton: Vernetzte Intelligenz (Networked Intelligence), Grazyna Fosar and Franz Bludorf, 2003.

This means that all DNA communicates with each other and by doing so forms the network. Humans naturally partake in these conversations when we are in a state of relaxation. Further information regarding this form of communication is given in chapter 9.

The medical condition tinnitus, a subjective ringing or tinkling sound in the ear, is a sign that someone is clairaudient. The condition can disappear when the sufferer starts to develop their clairaudient skills, but not every sufferer finds relief of this nature. Tinnitus and the natural loss of hearing doesn't affect the psychic working in this field; far from it, in fact it can enhance the gift.

Claircognizance (Knowing) There are three forms of knowledge: learning through experience (wisdom), academic and knowledge derived from inner or natural intelligence. Inner or natural knowledge emanates from memories of the sum total of our past lives[3]. All three produce learning curves which feed our intuition.

The combined knowledge is filed away in our long and/or short term memories in the brain and in the water element of our cells.

The human body consists of around two thirds water, because all cells are water-based. Water retains memory at a cellular level, so it will not be surprising to read that our bones, muscles and blood have independent memory banks to that of the brain.

This water based memory bank works in unison with both our cognitive and intuitive aspects. The water memory bank can be accessed through the endocrine system, which is responsible for producing hormones that regulate our bodies.

Hormones are known as the body's messenger for a very good reason. They transfer information from one cell to another. We have a never-ending rotation of knowledge moving around our bodies that we can draw upon. With every rotation the cells gather more knowledge. The circulation of

---

3   Francesca Rossetti : Psycho-Regression

this water needs to be regulated and that is the job of the hypothalamas. The interaction between the hypothalamus and the pituitary gland produces energy which can enable mind over matter. The knowledge can be accessed by psychics through their pineal, pituarity gland and hypothalamus to resurface past lives and retrieve inner knowledge.

Clairgustance (Taste) - five taste receptors, salt, sweet, sour, bitter, and umami have been idenitied on the tongue. Combined with the olfactory system, it is possible for a psychic to use these same taste receptors to 'taste' the essence of Spirit's presence.

Tasting the essence of Spirit can provide just as much information as working with clairvoyance, clairaudence or mediumship. Placing an object lightly on the tongue enables the psychic to access the pheromone template, which is left on an item belonging to a person after they die. Clairgustance is not widely used.

Clairalience (Smell) Olfactory and limbic system. The hypothalamus is a regulator and is responsive to light. It stimulates the the olfactory system. It also coordinates patterns of activity and assists in controlling emotions. It influences speech, (channeling) sleeping patterns (dream work) and eating (clairgustance).

Clairsentience (Touch) - The central nervous system is best viewed as the control centre of the brain. Its function is to automatically process information (sensory input) and respond accordingly (motor output). Also, the thalamus - which assists in regulating brainwaves - is responsible for levels of awareness and therefore enhances clairsentience.

Clairvoyance - The primary function of the lateral geniculate nucleus (LGN), which is a part of the visual system, is to process visual information received from the retina. During this process, part of the thalamus and the primary visual cortex are apparently activated and mental imagery results.

Although the function of the LGN isn't fully known, the information sent to and from the visual cortex may well produce the imagery that some people see in their heads. To you and me, it is our mind's eye, ajna or third eye. This process enables our ability to visualise (third eye clairvoyance). The pineal gland, known as the seat of the soul, also plays a role in clairvoyance.

It is thought that there is a connection between the LGN and the auditory system (clairaudience).

Mediumship – This is where a person wishes to utilize their body and/or mind to communicate with Spirit with the express purpose of receiving information. The person is known as the Agent or Channel and Spirit is known as the communicator. There are two types of mediumship, mental and psychic and it is possible for one person to accommodate both.   Mental mediumship is based on mental telepathy and takes place on a conscious level. It uses thought forms to receive and send information from the earth plane to the spirit plane and vice versa without using any of the five senses; only their sixth sense.

Physical or telekinetic mediumship is where the manipulation and the interaction between the medium and Spirit can be witnessed by others. Examples of this are an item falling from a shelf of its own accord, electrical appliances going off or on etc.

Mediumship uses many of the same attributes as those of a psychic; with telepathic mediumship using clairvoyance, clairaudience, clairsentience, inspired thought and automatic writing.

Telekinetic mediumship is when a person speaks on behalf of Spirit, is able to materilise objects from within the planes of existence, automatic handwriting (or typing), and trance work.

The above is a glossary and doesn't represent the full correlation between the physical make up of the brain and mind, both of which enable psychic ability.

I hope it does show how the body can and does accommodate what many call psychic phenomena. Far from being a phenomenon, psychic ability is as much a part of us as are our thought processes.

5. How Do I Prove To Myself I Am Psychic?

By accepting you are a psychic, you are placing yourself in a position where you can prove to yourself that you are. Below is a list of questions designed to do just that:

Questions
- Do you see things out the corner of your eye, in your peripheral vision, such as movement, lights or shadows?
- Can you picture an apple in your head?
- Do you see colours around pictures of people who you know are dead, or images that others cannot see?
- Can you walk into a room and pick up on an atmosphere or sit in a chair and have to move because you are not comfortable?
- Do you get unassociated thoughts coming across your head, and you think, "What did I think that for?"
- Are you light-sensitive?
- Do you think of someone and then meet him or her, or they phone?
- Do your dreams sometimes provide information?
- Do you dream of events that occur a few days or months later?
- Can you smell aromas that you know cannot be caused by anything in your house?
- Do you get different tastes in your mouth, (and you do not suffer from a medical condition that would cause this anomaly)?
- Do you know things without being taught?

The full answers can be found in Appendix III. If you have answered 'yes' to one or more of these guidelines then you are psychic. This means you are interacting with Spirit. Whether you realize this or not is immaterial. The more 'yes' answers, the wider the range of gifts.

If you have answered 'no' to all the questions then have a look at your possessions, which will give you an insight into how you are interacting with Spirit. Items such as a pack of Tarot, playing cards, crystals (including lead crystal and jewelry), books or magazines on the subject matter all reflect your Higher-self activities. Hobbies and interests do the same.

The next question you need to ask yourself is "Do you wish to develop your psychic gifts or not?" If you don't, fine - but remember that you are still psychic, because we all are. Therefore you may well find yourself reconsidering the issue later on in your life.

If you do decide to develop your gifts into abilities you become a practicing psychic. At first you may well experience a wave of enthusiasm known as a spiritual high, but don't try too hard or expect too much, nor put Spirit to the test. To do so shows that you may have tendencies toward being impatient or a Doubting Thomas, both of which are understandable but again, you run the risk of unwittingly closing yourself down.

Closing yourself down means you will be unable to sense the existence of Spirit despite the fact you are a practicing psychic. The problem will be of your own making so you will have to find the solution, which will reside within.

A Starting Point

Anything our brains can't make sense of is usually Spirit making contact. Spirit also uses the process of coincidences, synchronicity and correspondences to make contact through both rational and irrational thought. Whether these thoughts are rational or not is irrelevant.

Rational thought is dependent upon and influenced by life's

experiences, environment, culture and schooling and last but not least - the media. Most people can follow rational thought. Irrational thought is the counter-balance to rational thought and is active in the domain of the subconscious and pre-subconscious. This is the domain within which our instincts lie. We are not being rational when we follow our instincts.

Therefore, whatever information you do receive from Spirit needs to be put through the sieve of logic. If the information doesn't make sense, put it on the back burner and wait for more information or work with it until it does. Avoid becoming obsessive. If you start to feel instinctively that you are being driven, go with it, but make sure your hand is near the hand-brake of rational thought, and do not be too proud to use it.

By being open, aware and not dismissing spiritual messages as nonsense, you will in time prove to yourself you are psychic. When this day comes you should also be well on your way to identifying which direction you wish to take. To decide whether you wish to embrace your gifts and use them, embrace them and not use them or ignore them.

Taking Responsibility

At this stage it is time to stop and consider the consequences of which option you choose.

Whether you are single, married, in a partnership and/or have children, you need to stop and take time to review the situation. What you do with your life is of no-one else's concern, as long as your action or non-action doesn't adversely affect those around you.

If you are in a family unit, communication is paramount, but not before you have a clear understanding of what is involved in becoming a practising psychic and have already made your decision.

Should you find yourself receiving challenging feedback, remember at such times that you are an adult. As such you do not need anyone's approval so I suggest you don't seek it by default or otherwise!

It's all too common for people to discuss such matters with a family member, only to be dissuaded. It doesn't take much for the seeds of spiritual growth to be destroyed; this is because we are all far more impressionable than we wish to believe. Here are some of the responses you may well face:

"I wouldn't do that if I were you, you don't know what you are getting into"

"It's the devil's work"

"You - a psychic? Don't make me laugh"

"It's your PMTs/menopause"

"Midlife crisis"

"Maybe things are getting too much for you!"

Those who make such negative comments do so because either the change has made them insecure, they find your interest an affront to their belief system or they are scared. Although these are understandable reactions, you cannot ignore them, but you can avoid it or bring in damage limitation.

This can be achieved by being selective and, if necessary, economical with regard to the information you provide. You will get a very different reaction if you announce, "I am going to a personal development course. " Rather than "I am going to become a practising psychic."

Sometimes communicating through action rather than words is easier and more effective. This means the issue isn't open to discussion – you weave activities into your present lifestyle that will develop your gifts without mentioning it at all. We discuss this further in chapter 13.

Dealing With Fear of the Unknown

Fear is an instinctual emotion and we are all fear-based. The function of fear is to put us on alert mode. It gives us prior warning that something could be wrong and we become more aware of our surroundings. With fear comes courage, which enables us to face our fears.

Fear and courage keep us alive and these combined with

our ability to learn have enabled the human race to survive as long as it has. Recognising and understanding the importance of fear is the key to controlling it. This is despite the fact that sometimes fear is the appropriate response.

Fear occurs naturally when we go into the unknown. It falls into two categories; rational and irrational. Rational fear is when there is an obvious danger. Irrational fear is when there is no obvious cause for feeling feared. Our response under either circumstance is fight or flight, butsome people freeze.

One of the differences between humans and other life forms on the planet is our natural inquisitiveness, our ability to question and to move forward despite our reservations.

The ramification of this combination is that we can willingly place ourselves in dangerous situations. Why? - Because we have little if any choice. Our inquisitive nature demands that we do so because we have a never-ending thirst for knowledge. This thirst can only be quenched when we find the answers to our many questions, most of which start with 'What if...?' As a consequence we have developed various coping mechanisms that manage both our rational and irrational fears.

Some of these coping mechanisms are healthy and others are not. Belief is a coping mechanism, along with alcohol, cigarettes, drugs, lying, downtime, stress-management, music and TV. The list is endless. Bottom line, they all do the same job.

When committing to becoming a practicing psychic you need to know how you are going to cope whilst interacting with Spirit. Now would be a good time to identify what your coping mechanisms are. If you know or sense they are self-destructive, start developing ones that are self-constructive. Always bear in mind that ultimately, the only people who can help, harm or heal us are ourselves and knowledge alone negates fear.

Many people keep their fears at bay by wearing or holding an item they consider will protect them. These items are called talismans they can take many forms and usually represent a deity. Examples are: a crucifix, a cross, the Star of David, the pentagram, a shamanic medicine bag - again the list is endless. From a spiritual perspective it is the consequences of our own actions that we need protection from, not spiritual being.

The Role of the Joint Primary Emotions of Love and Fear

The joint primary emotions of love and fear are two different sides of the same coin. From the metaphysical viewpoint, the universal Laws of Duality show themselves in the human psyche through emotions.

These joint primary emotions within the human condition collectively become our survival instincts. Note: It is the fear and love of our selves not just of others that needs to be taken into account. All other emotions, including hate, are born from these two and are, for the purpose of this book, viewed as secondary emotions.

Fear is an ongoing state that rises and falls. The higher the state the more you fear, the lower the state the less you fear. Only a medical condition produces a totally fearless individual.

Focusing on fear feeds it and eventually very distressing distortions, which are produced by the mind, can occur. It has been long acknowledged that those who face their fears can move through them - by doing so they succeed in turning the coin from fear to love.

Love is a gift and it takes just as much courage to love as it does to face one's fears. Loving too much is just as unhealthy as fearing too much. It perverts, smothers, destroys, kills, distorts and misleads.

One way of keeping things in perspective is not to listen to or use fear-driven concepts, nor those that promise the earth or allow the love of the craft to consume you.

Both love and fear stop a lot of very gifted people from

identifying and/or developing their natural psychic gifts into abilities and reaching their full potential, both spiritually and personally.

Managing Fear

Paranormal phenomena occur when working with Spirit. Therefore psychics feel, see and hear things that other people don't. Some of these experiences will make sense and others will not.

At such times, rather than drawing upon our courage, we have a tendency to transfer the fears caused by what we do not understand onto our spiritual guides, angels and loved ones. Our rational mind picks up this irrational act and as a consequence statements like, "I am picking up negative/evil energy here" are made.

That negative energy is the embodiment of the fear energy that comes from the psychic. The lack of understanding is down to he or she having raised a guide etc., whose vibrational energy is higher or lower than theirs.

The two vibrational energies cannot work in harmony, so it is up to the person concerned to raise or lower his or her vibrational energy to avoid going into fear mode. Once this is done you will find the Spirit raised will be perceived as positive, not negative.

It is therefore advantageous to seek out a group of psychics within which such experiences can be discussed. Otherwise fear of Spirit can be developed and compounded, until a person thinks they are being possessed by the 'devil' or 'evil' beings.

We create archetypes when we are in either love and/or fear mode in order to try and make sense of what it is that we are witnessing. Archetypes are entities in their own right; they are messengers of, and from Spirit, their purpose being to assist us in understanding who we are. Ultimately, they enable us to become aware of the consequences of our own actions before we act. So let's get a few fundamentals clear:

37

- Spirit never guides us to where we are not ready to go, but our natural inquisitiveness does.
- Spirit always protects us from ourselves, but sometimes our fear can be so great that we feel disconnected from Spirit, even though Spirit's presence is greater in times of distress.
- Spirit never leaves us alone.

One of the best ways to manage fear is to SAY, not just think, 'ground, ground, ground' as soon as you possibly can. There is more about grounding in chapter 7.

Remember the emotion that balances fear is that of love. Love yourself and you protect yourself from yourself.

6. Interpreting Spiritual Messages

The simplest analogy I can think of to explain the process involved in interpreting spiritual messages is that of a three dimensional jigsaw puzzle. The complexities of such a jigsaw puzzle are determined by the number of pieces it has - so too with spiritual messages.

As with jigsaw puzzles, each message can come in any shape, size or colour and as such, one message on its own may or may not make any sense. Spiritual messages can take the form of a word, person, sentence, colour, animal, an archetype, a flower or simply a vision of white light or an indeterminable something. The only difference between jigsaw puzzles and spiritual messages is that they may also be invisible at times.

Those that consist of several phrases or a litany of sentences can evolve into channelling. It doesn't matter whether the messages are simple or complex, it takes time, determination, commitment, patience, awareness and observation to receive and understand spiritual messages. Sometimes Spirit contacts us for no reason other than because it can.

Spirit understands our human frailties, so to start with the messages may be simple but appear complex. As your awareness expands you should become more adept at picking up on them. Don't expect messages to always make sense. Accept that you may well receive some messages that will never make sense. This is because they have more than one meaning, usually three; since the three in one mystery applies to any 'one' issue or event.

Using the hyper-communication network, messages from Spirit come from outside of time into time and through the dimensions and inter-dimensions. It is the job of the Higher-self to receive and process the messages and there are a myriad of ways in which it does this.

Most people receive these messages when they are asleep. This is because when asleep, our minds have the ability to move through time space dimensions and inter-dimensions like a hot knife through butter. When we are awake, Spirit also uses subliminal contact through the use of co-incidence or what many recognise as synchronicity.

When working as a practising psychic, we automatically enter the ethereal plane to work dimensionally and/or inter-dimensionally. Therefore, having a basic understanding of dimensions is important, but it is not essential. For those who are interested, don't allow the dimensional and inter-dimensional aspects to faze you or let yourself become obsessed by them.

About Dimensions

We all function three dimensionally as a matter of course, and as such our world is made up of first, second and third-dimensional concepts. These concepts are embedded in the fourth dimension. The etheric plane is the interface between the third and fourth dimensions and is the doorway to the fourth and other dimensions. We all knowingly or unknowingly access the fourth dimension whether through meditation, going to a psychologist or thinking what to do next.

As far as spiritual development goes, our desire to work with Spirit places our minds in the fourth dimension. Practising and professional psychics make entering the fourth and further dimensions a career. As we spiritually evolve within our humanness, we are able to access the fifth dimen-sion and so on - it is a natural progression.

The more we work with Spirit in the higher dimensions, the greater our ability to interpret the messages and work with the three-in-one concept. This means that we are able to identify all three aspects that each message carries. The greater a person's ability to interpret the messages, the greater the ability he or she has to access the higher dimensions.

Accessing the dimensions is still in its infancy. Dr Michio Kaku's work within this field is well worth a read. There is a lot of similarity between his work and the long established concepts of metaphysics. We go into greater detail about dimensions and inter-dimensions in Chapter VIII.

Interpreting the Spiritual Messages that Lie Within the Human Body

From a scientific viewpoint the DNA/RNA are the building blocks of life - it makes us who we are. Holding genetic instructions, DNA determines the structure and controls the functioning of the body. The question that needs to be answered is: "Where do the instructions come from to do this?" From a metaphysical viewpoint, there are several answers to this question.

One is intervention, but another is to be found within the seven principles of Mental Transmutation, one of which is the the Principle of Correspondence. This principle embodies the concept of there being correspondences between the Laws of Phenomena and the physical, mental and spiritual planes. It could be viable that intervention would involve the Laws of Phenomena.

Correspondences arise when two or more different items infer the same thing and, by doing so, reveal hidden messages from Spirit. This process is based upon the concept that everything is connected and there is no such thing as co-incidence, as with synchronicity.

Correspondence is one of the keys used to unlock that which is held within the realms of metaphysics and is an essential tool of the psychic. It works with keywords derived from a myriad of sources. Once identified, the interpretation of the information is up to the individual that receives it.

A Key to Receiving Messages from Spirit is Silence

The nature of Spirit is to be found in silence. Therefore we cannot contact Spirit unless we understand the concept of silence. The sound of silence is heard through the absence of noise. It is used in many ways and for many reasons, but only in silence is the mind truly free.

When our minds are free, we are free. When we are free we can find the silence within. When we find the silence within we are in contact with Spirit, which only takes a nano-second. Once in contact, conversations with Spirit can take place.

Spirit uses silence to contact us, but doesn't need it to make itself known to us.

The Key to Deciphering Messages from Spirit

Messages and conversations with Spirit come in many forms and deciphering the messages can be a challenge. Sacred symbols, divination tools and keywords serve as codes and/or ciphers as well as reference points for gaining entry into the mysteries of working with Spirit.

There is a plethora of sacred symbols, divination tools and keywords simply because any item or word can be used in divination. Learn to read one divination tool and you can read anything. Why? An answer is because everything corresponds to everything else. How? The hyper-communication network provides us with the answers that are held within the Collective and that which is stored in our DNA.

Get the fundamentals right and what at first appears to be quite a complex process is simple once you get your mind working in a certain way. Any item or word can be chosen and by doing so, it is turned into a keyword.

The keyword chosen for this exercise is the word "dot". We already know that the "dot" is the sacred symbol used to describe the creation of the universe. Before the "dot" it was a time of primordial chaos, of darkness and clouds of gases from which the "dot" emerged. From it came the Big Bang and Life, as we know it. Considering this myth is thousands of years old, it has remarkable similarities with 'Into the Universe' by Stephen Hawking.

The "dot" also corresponds to writing and rules of language since it is used to end one sentence and heralds the next sentence. Below is a working example of a correspondence in motion.

- The dot is what is formed the second you put pen to paper, a finger to sand, a stick to clay, a quill to parchment or chalk to slate.
- From the dot comes the line that can be drawn horizontally, vertically or curved.
- The horizontal line can be read left to right or right to the left.
- The horizontal corresponds to the female energy • the left-hand side of anything represents the female aspect of the whole.
- The vertical line can be read from top to bottom or bottom to top.
- The vertical line corresponds to the male energy in its entirety • the right-hand side of anything represents the male aspect of the whole.
- When it is drawn as a continuous curve, the line stops being a line and becomes circle, which is made up of 360 degrees. The smallest circle is a dot.
- The circle represents unity and equality.
- When the circle is crossed over on itself, it forms the sign for infinity, • in the middle of which is formed a dot.
- From the circle comes the ellipse or a spiral.
- All lines and circles can be divided into three sections, each section representing past, present and future – in other words time.
- A three-dimensional circle forms a sphere, which corresponds to the planets, stars and female energy in its entirety.

- The sun, a star, corresponds to male energy • the moon to female energy.

All correspondences lead to another and this particular one leads to Mother Nature's abundance; the trees, flowers animals, rocks and insects etc., all of which also have a sacred function.

Because the function is sacred, the item used is a sacred symbol. This also applies to some utilitarian items developed by the human race, knives, cups, mirrors etc.

Sacred symbols in one form or another have accompanied the human race since time immemorial. Some have remained in their original format; others have developed into sophisticated divination tools such as the tarot and astrology. All sacred symbols represent correspondences.

When starting to follow correspondences we are able to see the simplicity and brilliance of Spirit and how it maintains contact with us. Any item can be used to represent and/or contact Spirit, or not, the choice is ours.

If you decide to follow the correspondences that apply to any word, a wealth of knowledge will be revealed. As to its relevance, that is another matter. During this process you may also find that nothing is as it appears to be.

Synchronicity

Psychiatrist Carl Jung first used the word to describe as he put it "temporally coincident occurrences of acausal events". In other words two similar or identical random events occur, the causes of which are unrelated. Synchronicity is an excellent example of the hyper-communications network in motion.

We have all witnessed synchronicity as well as played a part in such events. Synchronicity plays an invaluable role in the interpreting of spiritual messages. It is used to both confirm and a sign to act, or not.

"Do My Eyes Deceive Me?" "Yes, All the Time"

Once you have got used to working with keywords, correspondences and synergy you should able to see any normal everyday object in a different light. In the process you may well stumble across the concept of working hidden. When you are able to work hidden is when you eyes will stop deceiving you.

We all appreciate that with knowledge comes power and that working with hidden knowledge gives greater power - the greater the power, the greater the responsibility.

From the human perspective, working hidden is associated with the pre-sub-conscious, the sub-conscious, deceit and self-deceit. It also includes working behind the scenes, working in-depth and making one thing appear to be another. It is the Magician and Dark Side of the Moon energies, and the concept of 'Nothingness'.

Just because we can't see something doesn't mean nothing is there. Apart from the fact that the concept of nothingness is itself something, there is always something, because everything has purpose. Nothingness is no different.

Dark energy and dark matter are excellent examples of working hidden.

The more we work hidden, the more powerful we can become, the more likely it is we deceive ourselves. That is one way in which power can corrupt. We can only identify when we are deceiving ourselves when we mentally distance ourselves from our actions; we can do this by employing an invisible third party and by keeping our feet on the ground.

7. Keep Your Feet on the Ground

All those who walk the earth are earthbound and therefore grounded. That which flies is not earthbound and grounds only when walking on the earth.

Being earthbound enables us to draw upon the electromagnetic energies of the earth through our feet. These energies replenish our life-force energy in the same way food provides us with the energy to function.

Despite being earthbound our ability to ground fluctuates and being able to unground is a necessity. This is because our bodies are grounded and our minds are not. We use our bodies to ground our minds and cannot function to our full potential unless we do.

Being grounded means a person is able to keep their wits about them during times of crisis or ecstasy. A person who is grounded is realistically aware of his or her situation. They are therefore more in control of their reactions to the events going on around them. A person who is ungrounded isn't.

We all have the ability to consciously ground and unground ourselves. On occasion we can give permission for someone who is qualified in doing so, to ground us.

If you wish to develop and use your psychic abilities it is imperative that you understand the importance of grounding, since it enables quality time with Spirit. Without grounding you cannot contact Spirit without becoming physically exhausted in the process.

Most psychics find it challenging to maintain the discipline of grounding whilst working with Spirit, which is a strong, ungrounded force.

Grounding

Those who ground naturally are associated with conventional behaviour. These people feel far more comfortable on the earth plane. They have little or no yearnings for the cosmos. Such individuals usually provide the structure of our society, they are dependable and can maintain focus - the realists. Such individuals can develop into 'stick-in-the-muds', very stubborn and inflexible.

Here are some examples of a person who is suffering from being too grounded:

- Unable to react quickly
- Talking too deliberately
- Moving too slowly given the circumstances
- Can find change to be a threat
- Is usually set in his or her ways
- The mind freezes (minimal thought process) because the person is literally rooted to the ground.

Insecurity and aging are the two main reasons why people become too grounded.

From a metaphysical perspective grounding means that a person is able to replenish their essential life-force energies at will.

Becoming Ungrounded

Ungrounding is when the mind temporarily leaves the body from where it enters the etheric plane, through the second and third planes and then into the astral plane. The astral plane is the bridge between the lower and higher subtle bodies.

At such times, the physical body functions on autopilot. This means that the mind has semi-disconnected from the body and the body is using its own memory. As a result the person is not really aware of what he or she is doing, though they may think that they are.

47

Some people come into the world with little natural grounding ability. Such individuals are more cosmos aware than Earth aware, and it shows. They are associated with unconventional behaviour, or being eccentric and are usually flexible. These are the dreamers, the creative people whose heads are usually in the clouds. They do not need to be taught how to astral plane. Such people may find it hard to finish what they start or to take responsibility and deal with reality, in what ever form it takes. Here are some examples of a person who isn't grounded:

- Feeling dizzy.
- Feeling panicky.
- Thinking they are going to faint.
- Talking too quickly.
- Finding it hard to concentrate.
- Not thinking rationally, but being unable to stop it.
- Breathing too quickly.
- Shallow breathing.
- Not breathing at all.
- Rushing around but not achieving anything.
- Mind chatter (where you go over something again and again in your mind).
- The mind freezing because it is unable to function on body memory.

In extreme cases we actually come out of our bodies rather than simply semi disconnect in order to survive. We need to get back in if we wish to continue to function in an appropriate manner after the event.

Only the mind can muster enough energy to take us out of this and get us back in to our bodies.

Accidents occur when people do not concentrate on what they are doing. This is because the mind is literally 'else where'

One of the purposes of accidents is to ground people. Falling to the ground means a greater area of the body is on the ground and therefore it can assimilate a greater amount of grounding energy. Accidents are actually learning curves in disguise.

We also leave our bodies when thinking or wishing to remember. The process of remembering is a form of time travel that uses the mind, taking us back every time we think back in time and forward in time when we think of plans for the future. It is also the state in which we are able to receive ideas and inspiration.

From the metaphysical viewpoint, every time we are being drawn to look up at the skies, we are remembering, looking for and saying "Hi" to our Light-being States as our minds fly through the cosmos.

The Mechanics of Grounding

The function of the physical body is to house the mind and the Higher-self and grounding facilitates this task along with a good diet and exercise. The healthier the body is, the happier the Higher-self, the Soul and Light-being State.

If we stand on one foot we are less grounded than when we have two feet on the ground. If we are lying on a bed we are not grounded at all, but then we are usually inactive.

Most of the time the body naturally grounds itself by drawing up the Earth's energies from the feet into the legs, up along the body to the brain and exiting through the top of the head. By the time the energy exists, the grounding properties have been assimilated by the body at a cellular level and as it does so, this focuses the mind. Substances such as alcohol, drugs and some medications can cause people to become ungrounded.

The Mechanics of Grounding and Working with Spirit

Working with Spirit uses up a lot of physical and life-force energy. If too much of these energies are lost and not replaced, then physical, emotional and mental illness can eventually manifest. Physical energy (Energy C) is calorific in value and found in every cell of the body. It is replenished through breathing and with food, water and exercise.

Life-force energy (Energy B) is the spiritual counterpart of Energy C. Made up of cosmic forces and earth energies and is replenished through the process of grounding. It sustains the Higher-self, the Soul and Light-being state whilst they reside within its human host.

Energy B forms a core of energy at the time of conception. It is maintained throughout life and depletes with age. When the core is no longer, the physical body dies. The Soul, Light-being state and Higher-self is released from its' human host and is free to move onto its next stage of evolvement.

When we work with Spirit our initial response is to unground, it is an essential part of the process. In order to do this safely, we draw on both energies B and C simultaneously, otherwise the core life-force energy would be compromised and we would leave our bodies and totally disconnect from the host. Such is the force generated by Spirit. In other words Energy C enables Energy B to function in a healthy manner and vice-versa.

Therefore the more we ground whilst working with Spirit, the more rewarding the experience.

The physical response to people not grounding before during and/or after working with Spirit is that they usually feel hungry and/or thirsty. Some people eat instead of grounding themselves with the cosmic and earth energies because it stops the hunger pangs. Although eating is a valid way of grounding in the short term it can become unhealthy in the long term. Only the cosmic qualities of the earth's energies can be used long term to replenish Energy B and enable a person to ground and work with Spirit in a healthy manner.

How to Ground

The simplest but very effective way to ground is to take a deep breath and say or think: "ground, ground, ground". Do this until you start to feel more 'with it.' When speed is the essence, speaking is better than just thinking it, unless it isn't appropriate.

It is wise get into the habit of grounding throughout the day but not become obsessive about it. Some make of point of doing a daily grounding meditation; a good one is as follows:

- Visualise yourself in a forest with the sun shining through the trees.
- It is a warm day.
- You are in a happy frame of mind.
- You look around at your environment and are pleased and content with what you see.
- You take three deep breaths to breathe in the sunshine.
- You look down at your feet.
- You have no shoes on.
- You notice your toes and start to admire them and as you do you dig them into the soft warm soil.
- As you continue, your toes start to grow and turn into roots.
- The toe roots grow, digging further and further down into the earth until they come to the outskirts of its centre.
- The toe roots work through the magma, they start to feed on the raw energy of the Earth and as they do so, you may start to feel a warming sensation.
- The toe roots reach the centre of the earth where there is a large red, orange and yellow ball of flaming molten lava.
- Your toe roots wrap around this splendid warm ball of fire.
- As they do so, the colours start to be drawn up the roots into your toes, your feet, up your legs, into your hips, up along your spine to your neck, into your shoulders and arms, into your head, and out through the top of your head into the cosmos.

Stay in this meditation until you feel focused and calm. Then open your eyes and carry on with your daily routine. Another technique is to carry a black, brown or red crystal in your pocket or around your neck. Any such stones from the garden will do.

The Grounding Scale

Because we all unground naturally, we automatically adjust our grounding levels to accommodate whatever every-day situations we find ourselves in. The skill to grounding lies in knowing when to be grounded and when not to be. Table V: The Grounding Scale given below can be used to provide the information you need to know whether you are grounded or not.

Table V The Grounding Scale														
Ungrounded				Grounded Middle Ground					Too Grounded					
						I								
-1	0	1	2	3	**4**	**5**	**6**	7	8	9	10	10+		
Energy loss through lack of grounding				**Energy Being Replenished**					Energy loss through stagnation					

The numbers in bold represent balance. Number 5, underlined, represents perfect balance - something that is achievable, but never sustainable. It is also our default mode. Although our default mode is 5, on an uneventful but busy day the majority of us automatically function between 3 to 8 on the above scale.

Age is also relevant. Youth is associated with scale 1 to 3; middle age is associated with 4 and 7 mid-life; and senior citizens fall within the 8 to 10 range. We start to become ungrounded at 3 and the state of hysteria is 0 and -1. Minus 1 reflects life before birth, 10 Plus reflects life after death.

How to Read the Grounding Scale

The scale is to be used as a guideline only. Decide where you are along the scale by either using a pendulum, allowing your eyes to fall on a number or work with the first number that comes into your head. If you fall within the numbers 4, 5 and 6 you do not need to ground. Otherwise, take appropriate action.

- Before working with Spirit, commit to keeping yourself grounded as much as possible using the techniques already given.
- Decide how long you wish the session to last before you start working with Spirit.
- Visualise the Scale and ask which number you are. If you can't visualise or don't hear a number being given, use a pendulum or look at the scale and the number that stands out will mark your positioning.
- If you are still getting problems you are discovering that you are not grounded and do not wish to ground.
- If the number you are given isn't in the middle band, mentally move your energy along the scale until you know you are grounded.
- If the number 5 is given, or if you think you are in the middle, always double check.

As already mentioned, we are very good at deceiving ourselves. Most of this deceit takes place on a subliminal level, so when it comes to grounding, despite the fact it isn't healthy for us to be ungrounded for long periods of time, we often are. This is because being ungrounded can be and is an enjoyable experience - until the ramifications of not grounding come into play.

Maintaining Control

Whilst working with Spirit, keep an eye on your behaviour - without becoming inhibited or self obsessed. Visualise the

Grounding Scale and ask where you are along it intermittently throughout the session. It won't interfere and any necessary adjustment will have an immediate effect as long as it is your intention to ground.

If you forget to do this, it is an indicator you are not grounded. Try not to justify extending the time of the session. Your willingness to do so is a sign that you are ungrounded. If you decide to extend the session, do so, but ask first where you are on the scale and ground if necessary.

There will always be a reason why your Higher-self invites Spirit to visit you at an inopportune moment. This is not a problem if you take responsibility for your grounding. If the timing of a spiritual visit is not convenient or appropriate, ground immediately, and say or think 'no, please go away' then think or say 'ground'. Call Spirit back when convenient to you.

How to Un-ground

For those who feel more comfortable grounded, but wish to feel the joys of being ungrounded at scale 1 or 2, there are some crystals that are brilliant tools to get you going. Crystals work with intention. Both Moldavite and Labradorite are well known for their lift-off properties. Moldavite is an excellent mineral for this purpose, a kind of tektite formed by meteorite impact. Labradorite is found in the earth, is used by shamans and is associated with the cosmos.

If you decide to go down this route make sure you do it under controlled circumstances, not on the way home having just bought the crystals.

Remember expectations are rarely met, so don't expect miracles when you first practice ungrounding. If you have been grounded for xxx number of years it may take time to unground. There are always exceptions to the rule so you may go whoopee the first time you work with a crystal. Please remember to ground yourself after working with any crystal.

The Benefits of Grounding

By consciously monitoring your grounding levels you are taking responsibility for your own actions at a level you had not previously worked at. You are also training your mind through discipline. This means you are as in control of your self as any one can be. In time you will start to see subtle changes that can do nothing other than improve your lifestyle. Once you appreciate the skill of grounding you are well into your spiritual journey and can work on the astral planes at will, if you so choose.

8. Entering the World of Metaphysics, Cosmology and Cosmogony

Having an understanding of grounding, when to ground and unground, enables you to integrate the workings of metaphysics and its offshoots into your life. Metaphysics is a branch of philosophy that embraces the existence of Spirit whereas para-psychology, a branch of psychology questions it.

Cosmology, which studies the universe as a whole and cosmogony, which theorizes as to how the universe came to be, are both offshoots of metaphysics.

Working with Dimensions

In the world of metaphysics, dimensions, inter-dimensions and traveling through the dimensions of the cosmos are a fact of life. Such topics in the orthodox world are not fully understood but this doesn't stop us all from accessing the dimensions knowingly and unknowingly.

We pass from one dimension to another through anything that forms a threshold. Doorframes, two trees growing parallel to each other or standing stones placed in that fashion can all be used for dimension hopping. Doorframes and the like represent the separation from one area to another and correspond to the spiritual aspect of moving from one reality to another and from one world to another. They provide and represent the spiritual thresholds that exist within our minds and enable us to pass from one dimension to another.

From a metaphysical perspective, each dimension has a specific vibrational pattern, frequency and function. They are housed within the planes of existence, which is considered to be of various densities consisting of a subatomic nature and can be accessed using light or dark energy.

By combining Michael Sharpe's[4] work on dimensions with the metaphysical concept of DNA/RNA, I have developed a theory of how the first 15 dimensions and levels of density create our present reality.

For those who are interested in such matters, a table entitled, 'Correspondence of Dimensions and Levels and Their Psychic Definitions' can be found in Appendix II at the back of the book. It shows how the dimensions and levels correlate and has a list of densities and their associated function in relation to light into dark energy. The rule of thumb is the heavier the density the lower it is in the light spectrum until it progresses into dark energy.

Dark Energy

A very powerful kinetic energy, dark energy is behind all creation, which light energy creates. It surrounds and supports light energy and therefore holds the answers to the mysteries of life and death.

There is a lot of confusion regarding dark energy because it is associated with negativity, the 'devil' and evil. This is understandable since we cannot see in the dark, and therefore it allows our imaginations to run wild, which is scary if you don't understand the true purpose of dark energy. Step away from the negative press dark energy has and what you will find is the energy of bliss.

Once we have understood the truth of dark energy, we as Light-beings can move forward into our Dark-being state. In our Dark-being state we can become bliss rather than experiencing it in our Light-being state.

---

4 Michael Sharpe: The Book of Light

The Mind

The mind is pure energy and from this energy comes perception, imagination, sensations, emotions, intuition and thought. Like Spirit it is intangible, elusive and mysterious. Associated with light and dark energy, the mind is able to transverse these densities and by doing so travel through time and space and from one dimension to another. When the mind is out traveling, the self is active and functioning outside of its physical restraints.

We travel through the dimensions and inter-dimensions when we are doing guided meditations, visualizing, remote viewing, working as a 3rd eye clairvoyant, engrossed in an activity, day-dreaming and when in REM – the dream state at night. Therefore, we are all inter-galactic time travelers.

Proof that we travel in such a fashion is found in the form of a day-dream. The onlooker of a day-dreamer will see the glazed eyes. Unless drug induced or brain damaged, the eyes glaze naturally only when the mind is out traveling.

It isn't until someone raises their voice or touches the day-dreamer, that he or she 'comes back' at which time the person jumps. The jumping is caused by a person's mind literally jumping back into his or her body.

We have all found ourselves saying "you made me jump', more than once in our lives. How much and how often we jump is dependant upon how grounded we are. When our minds function outside of its physical restraints we are astral planing.

Whether consciously or not, we all surf the astral plane to retrieve information. We enter at the 4th dimension and from there work through the other planes of existence. The number depends upon which belief system is followed.

For the purpose of this book, as shown in Table VI, we travel to the 11th dimension and beyond. The 11th dimension is considered a gateway and enables access to the rest of the dimensions.

The Role of Light

Our ancestors understood the importance of light, whether it emanated from a fire, the sun, the moon or through reflection. As a consequence light is now irrevocably interwoven within our psyche. This is why many of us gravitate toward anything that sparkles.

Light has a psychological meaning and is used to describe those who wish to walk the path of enlightenment. The energetic meaning of light refers to kinetic energy, electromagnetic and electro-chemical energies found in the physical body.

Both meanings and relative functions of light energy as well as dark energy need to be taken into account when dealing with the dimensions, density and the role it has to play within the psyche.

It is my understanding that due to our present state of human evolvement, we perceive our natural state as that of Light. As such we use light to evolve from Light-beings into human-beings to experience the human condition. This is achieved by moving through the dimensions themselves as follows:

- Dimension 0 houses the energy that forms the etheric template.
- From this dimension the process of manifestation from Light-being to human being takes place.
- The etheric template begins to take human form as it journeys through the planes of existence.
- The final phase of the transition into a human being takes place in the 3rd dimension, which is embedded in the 4th dimension with an aspect of etheric plane acting as an interface.
- Within this interface is where the vibrational energies are compounded by gravity into matter as we know it.
- The shape and type of matter is dependent upon the etheric template.

The Aura

The aura represents seven of the planes of existence and is an external energy system that is associated with light, which is in itself quantum light. It is made up of forces that ultimately form subatomic particles. The auric field is made up of different levels of density of these subatomic particles which are referred to as subtle bodies.

An onion cut in half is a good description of what an aura looks like. The heart of the onion is the physical body with the surrounding layers being the subtle bodies. Each of the subtle bodies has a different colour, which can vary or change with the workings of the mind.

Auras appear as light coming from all around the physical body. It is not the physical body producing the light; it is the light that produces the physical body.

All matter has an aura, irrespective of whether it is organic or non-organic. This is because all materialized matter has an electro-dynamic energy field. Some see auras only around the head; this inspired artists to paint halos to depict Goddesses, Gods and Saints. Others see the light around the whole physical body.

The fact that some people can see auras without training proves the existence of the etherics. Such people are often unaware that being able to see auras is a gift. Instead they assume everyone sees what they see. This is not the case due to our uniqueness. Everyone has the ability to sense and/or see these energy fields but some of us need to be taught how.

For those who need to be taught to see auras, here is an exercise you can do to see them – don't try too hard and if it doesn't happen the first time, you may need to try every few days until you succeed:

- Prepare yourself by taking the phone off the hook and turning off mobiles.
- Clear your mind, focus on a person or pet that is standing or sitting still or a plant.
- Relax and semi-close your eyes.

- Wait for the energy field to show itself. If nothing appears after 15 seconds you may need to close your eyes a little bit more, without shutting them.
- Try again for 15 – 30 seconds and then stop.

To begin with, what you are looking for is very subtle traces, which may be intermittent around what you are focused on. As you practice, the aura should become clearer.

The colour may show itself or you may see what is called no-colour colour, which can only be described as a transparent haze. Auras can be photographed using Kirlian photography. Auras are translated using colour therapy.

An aura changes from second to second depending upon the task at hand. This means the photograph taken will only reflect what the aura was like at the time the picture was taken.

A procedure to sense the aura is to hold your hand an inch or so away from an object and close your eyes, if you think it will help. Wait for your senses to pick up on the electromagnetic field. You may feel a shiver, see something in your third eye, or undergo a 'hot flush' or some other slight or not-so-slight physical reaction.

The Chakras

The chakra system is an internal and external quantum light energy system that is also associated with light. Six of the seven major chakras are housed within the physical self. They are placed along the Sushumna, which runs from the base of the spine to above the head. This is where the 7th chakra and external chakras are located.

Chakras are interconnected with the aura; both are usually envisaged as independent concepts. Again, some people can naturally see chakras. The Earth, a living breathing entity in her own right, also has an aura and chakra system, as does this universe and the multiverse and all the associated dimensions and inter-dimensions.

Therefore, we are all children of the cosmos and metaphysics enables us to re-connect to our true source of being, which is that of Spirit. Isn't it deliciously simple?

9. The Importance of Thought

It is said that the beginning starts with any one thought, which is followed by action, thus creating reality. Therefore 'thought' is one of the tools Spirit uses to make itself known to us.

Both the chakras and aura accommodate thought in its purest form. Human thought existed long before both language and the written word became the codes for it.

Thought can pervade our very being, raise our spirits through humour and beauty or place us in the depths of despair through adversity and tragedy. Thoughts are private and hidden and can only come to light when written down or spoken. They come in many shapes, colours or sizes and are unique to each individual.

Thought is the ability to think and therefore it enables us to reason and make decisions that can be acted upon. It is nourished by knowledge and is supported by our six senses. Once acted upon, thought is responsible for creating a person's reality.

Thought will mean different things to different people. Some consider it to be the result of subliminal conversations between Spirit and the inner self. As these conversations surface to the conscious they identify themselves as thoughts. In other words we are what we think.

Last but not least it is Spirit's strongest connection to us and it is the vehicle used by the psychic whether or not he or she is practicing.

Thought and Cosmic Law

Where there is light there is law, cosmic laws, which turn the karmic wheel. Understanding and implementing two of these laws are fundamental to understanding thought.

The first is The Law of Cause and Effect and it determines how we live our lives. The scientific term for this law is for every action there is an equal and opposite reaction.

The second law that plays a major role in our evolvement is the Law of Attraction, which uses those we meet to improve ourselves. In other words through subliminal thought we draw those to us that reflect back what we need to learn about ourselves.

Remember these Laws, since thought, and thought followed by action, trigger both. This is because thought, both uses and produces energy to exist.

Thought and DNA

The questions are: What produces this intangible activity? Where does thought come from? The answer to both is that no one really knows, but it would appear that the answers themselves may lie in an idea originally conceived by Pythagoras in his concept; "the Human Octave of Energy" where the human body is naturally wired for sound.

Over the last couple of centuries, people such as John Newland, Crowley, Tesla, Robert Anton Wilson,[5] Leary and many others have developed this concept. The work undertaken by Russian biophysicist and molecular biologist Pjotr Garjajev found that genetic information found in DNA can be altered with sound. Further investigation has shown that it would appear that the human body sends out and receives intelligent messages. The sender and receiver is our DNA.

---

5 Robert Anton Wilson: The Octave of Energy.

Major works such as binary, the Mayan calendars, the I Ching, the Old Testament and our understanding overtones in music theory, to name but a few, are thought to be the result of this form of communication which is also referred to as the hyper-communicaton network. Identifying the correct frequency is the challenge.

The ramifications of this are enormous. It means that there is a possibility that we send and receive information through our DNA, which is stored in our minds and a byproduct of this process is thought.

Being a tool of nature, hyper-communication may therefore be responsible for organizing the behavioral habits of life forms, producing both our natural survival instincts as well as our intuition.

Within metaphysics, hyper-communication is called channeling, a valuable tool of the psychic. Channeling is an essential aspect of intuition and inspiration and it is the bedrock for communication with Spirit as well as other life forms that exist within the infinite multiverses.

Furthermore, scientists are now working on devices that can influence the cellular metabolism. Through modulated radio and light frequencies they are repairing genetic defects rather than the more 'traditional' invasive methods used of cutting and slicing DNA.

This work is simply confirming what the Shamans and other spiritual teachers of the pre mainstream religions have known all along; there is nothing more powerful than sound, irrespective of what forom it may take.

10. The Role of the Light-being

Where there is Light there are Light-beings. Light-beings are perfect, multi-faceted eternal beings of light with an intelligence and functioning beyond our understanding. They are individual entities in their own right and they contribute toward and work with the Collective and beyond, which is Dark Energy. Humans evolve through their Light-being state.

In the same way as our human state is the host for our Light-being state, so too is the Light-being host for our self-divinity.

They are active within all the dimensions and inter-dimensions and multiverses. Whatever image or concept the word Light-being conjures up for you, that will be the reflection of you in your Light-being state.

Although the Light-being state exists within each one of us, it also exists as an entity in its own right and has a parallel existence outside of time and space. Therefore our Light-being state exists before we are born as humans, it assists us whilst we are living as such, and we revert to our Light-being state when we have "shuffled off this mortal coil". It is the Light-being that enables us as humans-beings to aspire toward perfection.

There are various interpretations regarding Light-beings and this book is being written from the view that we are all Light-beings learning to be human, not humans learning to be Light-beings.

Light-beings transmute into human-beings so that they can learn about man's inhumanity and humanity to man. They achieve this through the process of reincarnation.

Those who contact their Higher-self through spirituality are able to become Light-workers in their human state. The Light-worker represents the Light-being state of an individual.

Try not to fall into the trap created by judgement that just because a person appears not to have consciously contacted his or her spiritual self due to their actions that are such that they offend the senses, that he or she is not a Light-being. They are. Their actions show that such individuals are walking a different path to you. It is the same path you either walked in a previous life, or a path to be walked in a future life.

From an esoteric perspective thought is a Higher-self activity since it forms a direct communication between our Light-being state and our human state.

We have deep-rooted memories of ourselves in our Light-being state and these can be accessed when functioning as Light-workers. These memories are activated by the symbols of Light-beings on the earth plane, which are the sun, the stars, a lighted candle, the moon or anything that glitters. Such memories usually surface as a collective memory, which has produced the concept of Life after Life, since from the Light-beings perspective there is no such thing as death, only a transition from one life to another. Each life may well take on a different form to the previous one.

This process also includes the parallel lives we live in any lifetime. These parallel lives are created by our decision-making, based on the opposite of or other options available at the time a decision is made. This means that when in our human state, we have multiple lives being lived by us concurrently within the past, present and future.

The common denominator is our DNA/RNA, a massive database that holds the history of existence and the cosmos as well as human history from the time we crawled out of the sea.

The DNA/RNA transmits information from one parallel life to another using the hyper-communication network. This information includes all the knowledge gained in past lives and the options open to us in future lives, including that of the Collective as a whole and beyond.

As humans, we draw upon the information held within this database which provides us with guidelines, pointers and information to assist us in whatever our quest is in any given lifetime as a human-being: Hence the existence of Cosmic Laws.

The Light-being state encompasses our starting point, our journey and our resting place - our true home. It is a state of all things and more which is integrated within each one of us. It holds all the answers to our human questions, understands our frailties and triumphs. Therefore, you are the one that has to decide, or not, whether you want to ask questions. If you do, it will be you who finds the answers, using your Light-being's guidance. Light-beings enable us to enter our Dark-being State and become Bliss.

The Light-being to Human-being Transition

Due to the dimensions, inter-dimensions, multi and parallel universes, it is possible for a Light-being to live more than one life simultaneously whilst keeping its own integrity within each active life.

Transition from Light-being to human being takes place when the egg is fertilized. The cosmic law of Cause and Effect comes into play. In other words, conception of a human being is the result of a Light-being shape shifting into the human form.

Cosmic Contracts

Now to expand upon what was mentioned in chapter I with regard to us choosing our lives before we are born. We plan a life in our Light-being state before we reincarnate into whichever life form we choose. This includes the positive experiences as well as the challenging ones, both in equal quantities. These choices are put down into what is called a cosmic contract that, along with cosmic agreements, caveats and blueprints, goes toward making a living four dimensional matrix, otherwise known as a life.

The contract is between us in our Light-being state and us in our human state. The purpose of the contract is to agree that in our human state we go through learning curves. As we undertake this task, we create karma, this is unavoidable until we transcend. Therefore the contract also enables us to balance the karma created, whether it be in the same lifetime or another.

Cosmic Agreements

Drawing up the cosmic contract involves other Light-beings who also wish to visit or revisit the Earth plane for their own purposes. Therefore cosmic agreements are made between all the Light-beings involved in the process. They produce the scenarios that enable the human condition to be experienced. Thus the detailed life of a human is mapped out and a cosmic agreement that applies to every action and non-action a person takes in his or her life.

As a consequence there is one cosmic contract and thousands of cosmic agreements to every lifetime. Despite what we may think as humans, we as Light-beings never renege on our contracts. Sometimes it will take more than one lifetime to complete a contract, hence déjà vu.

Caveats and Blueprints

There is a caveat to every cosmic agreement, that of Free Will. Free Will is sacrosanct to the human condition. It enables us to shape our own destiny as human beings whilst still adhering to the contract agreed between our Light-being and human state. The choices made are called blueprints and they are limitless.

The blueprints represent different realities and are formed from our own decision making as human beings. The greater the number of blueprints there are, the longer the life of the human being.

When all parties involved agree, the cosmic contract is signed, sealed and delivered as being the time of conception.

A Get Out Clause

There are those who cancel some of their contractual agreements and that is right for them. Obviously this is an issue associated with timing, since such cancellations will probably be reinstated later on.

A Life is Born

The ramifications of this are that we choose the family unit we are born into, the length of our lives and our sex. We also choose whether we are going to marry/partnership, or not; whether we are going to become addicts or not; whether we have a career, or not. And last but not least, how, where and when we to die and who, if anyone, attends our death (transition).

The choices made by us in our Light-being state are built upon knowing which existence will best serve its purpose.

In our human state we do not remember all of what or why we chose what we did as Light-beings. Therefore it is very difficult to accept that we are responsible for some of the distressing or traumatic things that happen to us. It is nigh on impossible for us to believe that in some lives we could behave like a Hitler or Stalin. But accept this we must if we wish to benefit from this way of thinking.

I cannot emphasise enough how imperative it is that when using this concept; it should never be used to justify any action that is associated with the challenging side of the human condition.

Once we are able to accept this we automatically place ourselves in a position of empowerment. That position is called taking full responsibility for our own actions, and the ramifications of those actions, as human beings.

With self-responsibility comes relative freedom. As someone once said, freedom is having the choice to choose which chains will bind us. True freedom only exists in our minds.

Death, Life after Death or Life after Life?

For some there is no spiritual life after physical death. These people believe that death is finite and after death we are no more on any level. This egoless belief has much in its favour since it encourages those believers to seize the day, every day. Others believe there is no spiritual or other form of life before conception, but there is a spiritual life after physical death. Then there are those who believe physical death doesn't take place at all. The physical body is transported in its entirety at an appropriate time.

Therefore physical death is seen as an integral part of life. Still it is also viewed as a transition, transmutation, transportation or disincarnation, where the human reverts back to his or her Light-being state.

From the Light-being state there is no death. There is simply eternity played out in different States of being of light - whether it is on the earth-plane or in another form of life that exists within the cosmos. This is because it is the Light-being's purpose to be, and it cannot be unless it experiences being. Being cannot be experienced unless it is – such is the concept of is-ness. From this perspective, physical death is the expansion of consciousness for both the human and the Light-being states.

From the human-being aspect, the question of whether there is life before life, life after death or nothingness raises many issues, one of which is that there are two certainties in life; the first being none of us will know if there is life after death until we die. The second certainty is we will all find out eventually.

The Human Conundrum

Psychics see Spirit in many of its forms. Logically, one has to ask that if there is no existence after death then why is it that psychics can see, hear or feel the presence of Spirit?

Many of those in the medical profession may well consider that a psychic is delusional and suffering from a psychotic condition. What goes against this argument is that approximately 99.9% of the population, including various members of the medical profession, have undergone at least one paranormal phenomenon themselves.

Logic demands that as far as the medical profession is concerned, 99.9% of the world's population is delusional. If 99.9% of the population is delusional, is it delusion?

From the psychic perspective, a state of delusion is called an altered state of consciousness that occurs with or without the stimuli of drugs. Altered states of consciousness are considered to be valid and important aspects of the human condition and those who are practicing or are profes-sional psychics recognise and work with this gift. Both viewpoints are important because they both have a role to play.

Those who are sceptical of psychic phenomena are another sector of society whose role is important to understand. The psychic and the sceptic are two sides of the same coin.

The sceptics are a reflection of the sceptic that lies within all of us. It is this doubt that, when managed properly, keeps practising and professional psychics from entering permanently a state of delusion that does trigger psychosis and will need medical intervention.

11. Where Does Religion Fit Into All this?

It would appear that religion in one form or another is a need within the human condition. Due to our individual uniqueness, we need different ways of expressing our spiritual beliefs, even if that belief is agnostic or atheist. Therefore religion, in all its forms, is a celebration of our individual perception of life and our search for truth.

All the religions of today have their origins in shamanism, the first religion. It may be helpful to think of shamanism as being the roots of family tree, with all the other religions spanning/extending out from it.

A person doesn't have to disassociate him or herself from religion to be a practicing or professional psychic. On the other hand, a psychic's religion should not be imprinted onto the reading. As long as respect is given to another's beliefs there is no conflict of interest.

It may be worth noting that all religions were - and still are - started by those who have had a profound spiritual experience. In other words he or she saw, heard, felt or otherwise interacted with Spirit. And thus the seeds of a new religion are sown. Some become established and others do not. New religions can be used to measure how we are evolving.

What Makes Religion?

From the psychic's perspective, irrevocably interwoven into the different religions is the influence of the environment within which a community lives. Different environments hold different challenges for the community that need to be met in order for it to survive. It is the environment that forms a culture and the people that develop it. Some religions reflect this culture, others do not and some are adjusted to do so.

These cultures are expressed through natural intelligence, which develops knowledge, and that in turn when lived produces wisdom.

Natural intelligence is produced by everyday events, which in turn dictates how we act or react to any given situation. Natural intelligence is the precursor of academic intelligence.

Look closely and you will be able to trace the invisible footsteps of Spirit throughout this process. Whether it is in the form of Mother Nature or an all knowing and seeing archetypal figure doesn't matter. It is Spirit and only Spirit that has such power to manifest itself as a religion or belief.

Therefore, when you strip away the human interpretations and embellishments found within all the scriptures of all the religions, you will see that they all have the same message. Fundamentally, this very simple but all-important and all-all-embracing message is revealed; by respecting yourself and each other, you respect Spirit. Respect Spirit and you receive its unconditional love.

Fundamentally, a very simple but all-important and embracing message is revealed, which is by respecting yourself and each other, you respect Spirit. Respect Spirit and you receive its unconditional love.

Therefore religion is simply one of the vehicles Spirit uses to make itself known.

Spirit is also to be found in such areas as quantum physics, physics, play, singing, biology, art, music, design, poetry, medicine and politics – you name it and it is a face of Spirit. In other words Spirit is Life and its work is seen in the living as well as representing the dead.

12. Contacting Spirit

Although we are in constant contact with Spirit on a subconscious level, it has been necessary for us to devise ways of contacting Spirit on a conscious level. One way is through prayer and another is through divination. Both are ancient ways of conversing with Spirit, they both have their place and one is no better than the other. It is simply a matter of what suits the individual the best.

Prayer can be a deliberate practice and take a form of an incantation, a hymn or a creedal statement. It can also be made up on the spot or take the form of what appears to be someone who is talking to themselves, or mind-chatter. Chanting is another form of prayer as is the prayer wheel and prayer flags all of which are commonly used spiritual practices. Then there is the prayer that takes the form of silence.

Divination is also a form of prayer. There are as many different forms of divination as there are religions. It could be argued that religion is a form of divination since the word is a derivative of Divine.

In the past, psychics were known as diviners, oracles, wizards, the cunning (skilful) man or woman, fortune-tellers, prophets and soothsayers. The list is endless. At one time such people were highly respected and formed an integral part in society. Psychics still play an important role in present day society and until recently there has been little acknowledgement of this.

The reticence of society as a whole to recognise the role of the psychic is that some within the mainstream religions who still consider the art of divination to be the work of the 'devil'. Therefore psychics are often considered by hardliners within these religions to be working for the devil. What counteracts this misconception, as already mentioned, is that there are plenty of psychics who also practice mainstream faiths.

Divination

Divination or instinctive foresight falls into three categories. It is important to understand that we all have a natural tendency toward all three categories, which are:

- Intuitive - considered to be the foundation of divination, it is used by all psychics and mediums in one way or another.
- Inductive - information is obtained from Spirit by reading 'signs', whether it be through the elements, direction (north, south, east, west, above and below), birds, animals and nature in general.
- Interpretive – information is obtained from Spirit through dreams and correspondences and then aligned to astrology, dream interpretations, numerology, tarot, colour, runes, crystals, an onion, eggs, bones, shells – whatever.

Every culture will have its unique form of divination, which is channelled through priests, Shaman, witch doctors, medicine women etc.

It is their responsibility to perform the rituals associated with the type of divination they represent.

A practicing psychic is also a diviner and it is up to him or her to decide how they wish to portray their gifts.

Archetypes

Prior to monotheism, both the positive and challenging sides of human nature were depicted by, gods, goddesses and archetypes. The modern day archetypes that represent the human psyche in the west are God and the devil.

Irrespective of all the belief systems, the emergence of these 'mythical' figures are the result of people trying to understand who they are, including their challenging side.

In psychological terms, the challenging side is the 'Id'. From the psychic's perspective, the Id is an aspect of self that provides balance to the Light-worker self. The Id is associated with an essential unorganized part of the personality and is therefore an essential part of the spiritual self. Without it we cannot evolve.

The Id's function is to avoid pain and happenings that are not pleasurable. Such experiences equate to and are associated with illness, danger and physical death. It succeeds by producing the drive for us to find water, food and to reproduce. Our species cannot exist without it. The Id is beyond morals and ethics and has to be. Working through our instincts, the Id is fear based and therefore produces the challenging side of the human. When unbalanced and unchecked, it is inhumane.

The counter balance to the Id is the ego and super ego, both of which aim for perfection. Combined they make up the human psyche. The ego is structure, intelligence etc., and the super ego houses Spirit. Spirit works through our instincts and by doing so supports our positive side and counteracts the Id. It is the ego's job to make sense of it all.

The Id and super ego reside in the unconscious and ego is the conscious self. Fear feeds the Id and therefore influences our actions. Therein lies the dichotomy. We cannot live in a continually harmonious and peaceful existence because of our very nature. We can aspire to achieve this goal and by doing so reach it.

Through our attempt to understand our natures we have at times, and by default, fed the Id with horrendous consequences. The truth of it is that our fears are released on anyone who is perceived to be different. So, it is not surprising that we find ourselves living in a fear driven society.

It is human nature to create a mythical scapegoat to blame, namely the devil. Once created, the concept of the devil developed a life of its own and now represents all that is negative about the human condition.

What is laughable, if it were not so tragic, is that it isn't the external mythical devil that tempts us; it is the Id that lies within. By blaming an archetype for our own actions it causes confusion. When confused we are not taking responsibility for our own actions.

This contorted way of working is why Light-beings choose to be human. Only by being human can they experience the continual interaction between the Id, the super ego and ego.

Human Evolvement

The first phase of human evolvement is to understand and learn to control the Id. Divination in all its forms enables people to seek spiritual guidance when they need it to achieve this goal.

The next phase of human evolvement is self-empowerment. As the human race evolves, it self-empowers. One of the consequences of the First and Second World Wars was the emergence of individualism, the self-empowering individual.

As a result, the needs of the individual have begun to be recognized, respected and then cemented in law giving the individual certain rights.

Individualism is necessary if we wish to self-empower. Self-empowerment is the greatest wealth any of us can ever possess. This is because as we self-empower, we can negate the fear we have of ourselves.

A knock-on effect of individualism is that, in general terms, control by both the state and religious bodies is challenged and therefore weakened. It is the responsibility of both state and religion to meet those ever changing needs of its people.

This is unavoidable if people are to take responsibility for their actions and by doing so become empowered. Individualism and self-empowerment don't necessarily lead to a breakdown in society, as some fear. They can lead to a cohesive society built on co-operation, if the powers that be allow it.

13. Blindsides, Self-empowerment and Self-discipline

Karma encapsulates the issues of action and reaction/cause and effect. For those who may not yet have come across these Buddhist and Hindu mindsets, karma is essentially the concept that good or bad actions will bring upon oneself inevitable results, either in this or another lifetime. In other words, what goes around comes around.

The more we learn about Spirit, the more we reveal the quintessential qualities of our characters and are able to recognise our righteous duties - referred to as Dharma.

The characteristics we are not aware of are called blind-sides. We are blind to many of our positive characteristics as well as our challenging ones. The procedure of identifying blindsides and balancing karma is unavoidable - they go hand in hand

A part of spiritual development is identifying these blindsides and by doing so enabling self-enlightenment. It is amazing what can be seen if time is taken to have a good, long hard look in the metaphorical mirror every now and then.

Identifying and dealing with blindsides enables us to become more understanding and less judgemental of those around us. It is easy to become self-obsessed or go into denial at times, but that is all part of the journey. Going into denial is positive since it is the sign that a 'blindside' has been exposed. Staying in denial only prolongs the process.

This work is imperative for those who do not wish to become hypocritical psychics. Those who have the ability to laugh at themselves have an easier time of it than those who take themselves too seriously.

Self-empowerment

Self-knowledge enables us to separate from the so-called norm and move toward individualism, which lies outside of the norm. To begin with, this separation may not be noticeable but it's there. You may well run the risk of distancing yourself from those who are close to you if you don't manage the process with care.

Through self-knowledge you are discovering who you are and as you do so you become self-empowered. Others may well perceive this self-empowerment as you changing into somebody they can't relate to anymore. You are not becoming someone else; you are becoming yourself.

This process can cause confusion and concern in others - why? Because you are becoming fulfilled, empowered, purposeful, grounded and focused, not by using the orthodox channels but through working with Spirit, an intangible, unseen force.

As a consequence you may well also become a catalyst for some of those around you and highlight other people's blindsides by default. This can be difficult, but it is an essential part of self-empowerment and does need to be managed. If managed well, it is a brilliant way of working with personal boundaries whilst highlighting blindsides in the processes.

You may suffer from self-doubt and feelings of guilt at times but this is all part of the process. By maintaining focus on your goal, which is to self-empower, you are providing those around you with a very positive example of a person who is getting in control of their life.

Those who cannot tolerate others who are in the process of self-empowerment are on a very different but just as important path.

Blood is thicker than water, and very few people experience long-term issues within the family. At the end of the process you will find yourself reforming friendships or finding new friends.

Nevertheless, it is up to you to bring in damage limitation as you self-empower. One way of doing this is to first identify who you should and shouldn't be sharing your thoughts with. To do this you use the 'need to know' principle and common sense. Here are some guidelines that may assist with this very personal and complex situation.

- Raise your interest in metaphysics with those that you know will be sympathetic, not a devotee of some of the major religions unless you know them well indeed. By exercising caution you are not only respecting their religious beliefs but also respecting your own.
- Assume nothing. If there is someone who you consider is open to discussing metaphysics, ask if he or she watches T.V. programmes about psychics or ghosts? If the answer is "no", they may well be waving a red flag and you should consider changing the subject onto something like crystals. If the response is "yes" the amber flag has been raised, at which time you ask: "have you witnessed any psychic phenomena?" If the response is "yes" again, the person is probably waving a green flag, so continue, but with caution. Always remember, it is one thing to watch 'Most Haunted' on the T.V., it is another to meet a practising psychic.

Spiritual Highs

Spiritual Highs (SHs) occur in, and are the mainstay of, every mindset or religion and denote that enlightenment of an individual has taken place. An SH can last for minutes, hours, days and in some cases weeks. The effects of an SH can be a life changing event, or not.

The function of an SH is to enable enlightened information to be received from Spirit in order to gain understanding, insight and clarity. As a consequence they can be joyous, electrifying, liberating and awe inspiring. SHs can encapsulate the essence of unconditional Love.

81

They occur due to a chemical reaction within the brain, which responds to interactions with Spirit. As a result, the person undergoes an altered state of consciousness, which can provide a fundamental change of perspective based on the power of love, knowledge and compassion.

Those who have consciously interacted with Spirit in this way often feel the need to 'convert' all those around them, and psychics are no different. Evangelism is an understandable reaction to such an event. Take care, such moments are intensely personal, and only those who have witnessed or felt them can appreciate your words.

Some people may well undergo a down turn, which can leave them feeling lost and doubting that anything happened in the first place. Rest assured, it did.

These downturns are a perfectly natural and healthy reaction since SHs are not sustainable. If both responses are left unchecked at their respective zeniths, unnecessary problems can arise. It takes discipline to regain balance.

SHs unground, and it is important to develop the self-discipline to ground as quickly as possible after the event. Before grounding takes place, the person may think they are behaving in a perfectly rational manner. From the metaphysical sense they are. From the orthodox viewpoint, onlookers may well consider there is reason for concern.

Only by using self-discipline to ground throughout and after an event can you control your emotions and gain true benefit from the experience. Otherwise you may well go into fear mode during an SH and lose the moment.

Discipline

Most of us do not like being disciplined by others and we rebel against it, as we should. Our views upon the subject are usually dependant upon what type of discipline was endured during childhood. If challenging, it is important to move through those experiences by employing the concept of balancing karma and going through learning curves.

Discipline is another one of the vehicles used to enable human evolvement and to attain spiritual enlightenment. It not only sows the seeds for rebellion, it also creates structure.

There are two categories: being disciplined by others and self-discipline. Both categories enable the same sub-categories; the discipline to do something and the discipline to not do something. Life teaches us about self-discipline through personal experience.

Self-discipline is the key to a productive and healthy orthodox as well as spiritual life. We all have the ability to discipline our selves to do something and to not do something.

Keeping a Perspective

It is vital to gain and maintain perspective when functioning as a practising psychic. This can only be achieved by developing a balanced lifestyle, where you have one foot in the orthodox world and the other in the mind, body, Spirit sector of society.

There are several ways to introduce yourself to this sector, one is to find a dedicated 'Mind, Body, Spirit' shop and wander around it. Pop in several times to get used to the ambiance. Many of these shops are also hubs where local complementary therapists, psychics, Light-workers and pagans frequent or work. Some of the owners keep a notice board advertising various activities.

When wandering around, the rule of thumb is that whatever takes your eye is where you need to start. If everything in the shop takes your eye, please remember self-discipline. It is very easy to get financially carried away, especially with the crystals. Once started don't be surprised if you have an overwhelming thirst to find out more - this is all part of the process.

A measured way of introducing yourself to metaphysics is by surfing the net. Any good search engine will bring you up a wealth of goodies if you enter 'psychics', 'clairvoyants', 'Tarot', 'numerology', 'Mediumship', 'channelling' or 'walk-ins' - just for starters. There are plenty of respectable dedicated interactive websites[6] who provide a wealth of information and personal insight into all aspects of spirituality. Needless to say, safety guidelines need to be adhered to - there are a lot of oddballs out there and quite a few can be found in the 'Mind, Body, Spirit' sector.

If you are thinking at this point, 'I will give it a try and see what happens', be aware. Expectations are rarely met, and whether you realise it or not, "giving it a go" means you could also be unwittingly testing Spirit and Spirit isn't for testing. At the same time it is important to make an informed decision and no one can do that unless he or she is prepared to put in the time and effort to do so.

For some, there may be a myriad of different reactions and emotions that are raised during this process. They are an essential par for the course before making that final commitment to Spirit.

---

6 www.thespiritguidesnetwork.co.uk

14. Commitment to Spirit

The third step along this journey is to consciously contact Spirit and by doing so, you accept you are psychic. The fourth is to understand the principles of spirituality and metaphysics. The fifthstep is to decide whether you wish to commit to Spirit on a conscious level. If you wish to see what you are committing to, look in the mirror.

The decision to consciously commit to Spirit can take time or be immediate, depending upon the circumstances. It can come subtly or in your face; directly or indirectly, whether it is through Divine intervention or a traumatic or tragic experience, all of which leave a person knowing that there must be 'something more'.

The 'something more' is usually hidden in plain sight, so allow your life as it stands to guide you. Correspondences can be used to expose what is hidden and the starting place is with what you do or would like to do as a career or hobby within the orthodox world. Examples of such correspondences are given in Table VII.

Table VII Occupation Correspondences	
Profession/Hobby	Spiritual Counterpart
Artists	Colour therapy
Architects & Builders	Crystals and/or sacred geometry
Crosswords	Runes and/or the I Ching

Authors	Channelling/automatic handwriting
Media	Tarot
Mathematicians	Astrology
Accountants	Numerology
Homemakers and Chefs	Alchemy
Mechanics	Sacred Geometry
Pilots	The Planetary Grid
Farmers	Topography
Electricians	Spiritual Electricity
Engineers	Geomantic Power Sites
Plumbers	The Ethereal Waterways
Actors & Singers	Archetypes

This table should not be used to dictate where you start. You might be an artist and have no interest in colour therapy. Alternatively, you may never have picked up a brush in your present life but are drawn to go on a colour therapy course.

As a whole, we understand very little about our orthodox lives and how they correlate with our activities in Spirit and our corresponding purpose within the Collective. We do know that whatever we do in the orthodox world affects what happens within the etherics, our parallel lives, dimensions and inter-dimensions. We know this because everything is interconnected, if it were not, the concept of correspondences would not exist.

The more we learn to read the correspondences, the more our contact with Spirit strengthens, as does our commitment to being a practising psychic. It is at this stage we become more at one with ourselves.

Where you start can often define your elementary psychic abilities. Although this definition will evolve and change as you develop, the process itself is a commitment to Spirit. It is also an excellent way of identifying the knowledge you have brought in from past lives.

Commitment to Spirit can be, is and will be fun so don't give yourself a hard time by turning it into a chore. Don't worry if you have a few false starts, it is an essential part of the process, since they are one way of getting you to where you need to be. Acting as indicators of how confident you are, false starts also highlight your ability to self-sabotage due to fear of failure or success. False starts can occur due to past life knowledge resurfacing or when you are drawn to another course having only just started one.

Turning your spiritual wealth into financial wealth is a voyage of self-discovery, and therefore it needs to be seen in that light. So you may end up doing the complete opposite to what you originally started out to do.

15. The Path of the Practising Psychic

Irrespective of the different types of psychic there are, fundamentally everyone falls into two categories - academic or intuitive. Both categories are just as important as each other. So the next step along your journey is to identify which category you fit into. If you don't know which category you fit into, you may well close yourself down unless you can accommodate both ways of working.

Read through the following categories to decide what best describes you. You do need to be completely honest with yourself when making your choice.

1. You have strong instincts and you follow it.

2. You have strong instincts, but you ignore it.

3. You do not consider yourself to be instinctual.

4. You didn't consider yourself to be instinctual but are now becoming so.

5. You know you have been psychic since a very early age.

6. None of the above.

If you have identified 'yes' in numbers 1, 2, 4 and 5, infers you are an intuitive and numbers 3 and 6 that you are an academic. Identifying with all 6 usually means you are using both techniques.

The Intuitive

Being an intuitive rather than an academic psychic means you are already using your intuition in every day decision-making. You may be aware or totally unaware of this and whether or not you dismiss or go with your instincts it is not the issue. The issue is, you are intuitive.

Other indications are that you prefer to rely on your memory rather than write a list or to look at films rather than read the book. All dyslexics are intuitive, but that doesn't mean that they are not academic in the orthodox world.

You may not be drawn to look at the academic side until you start to develop your skills and even then you may find there is an element of it not being necessary.

The Academic

Being an academic psychic means you may well follow your instincts in exactly the same manner as an intuitive, but you prefer to learn from books to contact with Spirit. You will be drawn to write a list rather than rely on memory, and prefer to read the book rather than watch the film adaptation of it. Just because you lean toward being academic, it doesn't infer that you are an academic in the orthodox world.

Identifying which Path

Identifying that you are either an intuitive or academic psychic doesn't mean you will stay in that category. People evolve from being an intuitive to an academic and vice versa, most combine both.

Unfortunately in this qualification-obsessed world, many people assume that an academic is 'better' than an intuitive psychic, this is not the case. Then there are some within the psychic profession who consider an intuitive is 'better' than an academic. This is also not the case, since one is no better than the other.

When you have determined which type of practising psychic you are, you can then focus upon identifying your path. For some this will be easy, simple, for others confusing and challenging.

One way of doing this is to identify the path that has led you to where you are now. Below is a very basic list of circumstances, also known as Paths of Circumstance. Choose one or more paths that you can relate to:

- Your desire to find out more is so strong that you have no choice.
- You are concerned about a lack of finance.
- Your life is falling apart for 'no apparent reason', i.e. break-up of a partnership, redundancy, and emotional crises.
- You are, or have been, suffering from ill health.
- You know there is something more but don't know what.
- You are undergoing a lifestyle change.
- You feel it is time to develop a gift you have always known you have had.
- All of the above.
- Path not listed.

The path that stands out the strongest for you is the path that has taken you to where you are now and which will have led you to the crossroads.

The Metaphorical Crossroads

Although obvious, it is worth taking time to reflect upon life's crossroads, where two roads meet. Turning left or right is moving sideways and going straight ahead is moving forward. Standing at the crossroads is reflecting and turning around and going back is returning from whence you came. Cross-roads are also the place where people can identify that they have gone around in a circle.

Metaphorically, crossroads means decision-making, they are also associated with the concepts of: avoiding repeating the past in the future, getting stuck in the present and recognising that there are always opportunities ahead for you.

To be at a metaphorical crossroads also indicates it is time to stop and reassess. This is because you have come to a turning point in your life and you are being presented with several unknown options. The option you do know is the decision making that took you to where you presently stand, and that path is associated with the past.

How you approach a crossroads determines how best you manage the situation. To move forward without first stopping and looking left or right infers recklessness. Stopping and hesitating infers indecision.

Turning left or right may well take you eventually to where you wish to go, whereas moving forward will take you there directly. If you stop at the crossroads and don't make a decision, obviously you don't go anywhere.

The Psychic's Crossroads

Knowing whether you are an intuitive, academic or both can help you decide where you wish to start your spiritual journey, and it means you have come to a crossroads. By doing so you have created a variation of the metaphorical crossroads, the psychic's crossroad. Therefore the road on the left corresponds with female energy and the right corresponds with male. It is worth noting that this could also infer the left turn corresponds with intuitive psychics and the right with academics.

If you turn left or right at the psychic's crossroads you are using your skills but not developing them. If you go straight over the crossroads you are making the decision to develop your psychic abilities and as you do, you start to walk the path of the practising psychic. This path will take you to another crossroads where you will need to stop and decide whether you wish to train as a professional. Here are some guidelines for you to consider or be reminded of:

- Walking your spiritual path needs to become a way of life if you wish to receive the maximum benefit.
- When it comes to the concepts of your spirituality, you are always right but only when it is applied to you, not another.
- For every one of your actions there will be a reaction.
- When you forget about the consequences of your own actions you are developing an essential learning curve.
- Don't expect or need others to agree with you.
- Nothing can help, harm or heal you but yourself.

The Metaphysical Crossroads

Metaphysically, a crossroads can represent being between two worlds, neither in one place or another whilst being in all places at the same time. All the paths can be interpreted as being androgynous.

It's the Journey not the Destination

It has long been considered that all life's paths lead to the same destination; therefore it isn't the destination that is important. It is how the journey is undertaken that needs to be focused upon.

The journeys that start with a vision usually have no navigational aids or are broadly mapped out. Here are some guideline analogies to bear in mind:

- Cul-de-sac, these are also resting places as well as dead ends.
- Crossroads and junctions are for stopping, reassessing, and decision-making.
- Roundabouts are for giving options, with the risk of going around in circles.
- Motorways are for when you are focused and know where you are going.
- There are lay-bys and hard shoulders for resting.

- 'A' roads are for those who wish to take their time.
- 'B' roads are for those who wish to explore.
- Side roads are for the intrepid explorer.

Long journeys have to be taken in stages. These stages are called stage posts. Although you may have started off with a final destination in mind, you may well change your mind along the way.

So when you reach a crossroads, you need to:

- Rest
- Review
- Prepare

Resting enables you to refuel. Reviewing is essential, since you need to know how far you have come to get an idea of how far you have to go. Preparing is taking responsibility and by doing so you are showing Spirit that you are eager to move forward.

16. Seven Rites of Passage of a Psychic

A ritual that celebrates a change in a person's social status usually denotes Rites of Passage (RoP). Such celebrations are usually marked by an event, such as a baptism, a wedding, a Bar Mitzvah or a funeral.

Life is made up of various RoP, which are usually formed by a sequence of events. Some of these events are challenging, whilst others are pleasurable. With time and experience you will recognise an RoP before you enter into it and therefore take it in your stride.

Generally speaking, all RoPs hone a person into being able to meet their full potential and then exceed it. During this process our blind sides are usually exposed and we become aware of our true potential as human beings.

All RoPs have a spiritual element to them that applies to the well-trodden path of a psychic. They enable us to come from a mindset where we are not in conscious contact with Spirit to one where we are. RoPs enable us to witness and feel what was considered to be nonsense as it is transformed into an individual's 'Truth'. This is a very empowering process to undergo, since it teaches us tolerance of ourselves. Only by tolerating ourselves can we tolerate others.

When working with RoPs, try to remember that there is no such thing as 'getting lost on your journey'. We are never 'lost', although we may feel like it at the time. We are simply going through a process that teaches us about the complexities of time and space.

Whether we like it or not, in this dimension, everything has its own time and space in which to unfold. There is little we can do about that as human beings other than to understand, accept it and trust in ourselves.

There are three phases to an RoP: the initial phase is separation, which is self-explanatory. The second is a state of liminality, which for this purpose represents the metaphysical threshold, an in-between state of transformation. The third phase is a re-incorporation after transformation.

Identifying when you are in an RoP is not always easy. A pointer is that if you find it too difficult to identify what is happening in your life, you are usually in the first phase.

If you decide to refuse to enter the second, well done you, because this can mean you are developing your ability to stop, reassess and question. Don't be surprised though if after you have finished that process, you find yourself having to deal with what you thought you could originally avoid. This denotes you are ready to enter the second phase.

The second phase is doing what you know needs to be done, bearing in mind the consequences of your actions and despite the fact you don't want to do it.

Having done it, you enter the third phase. This is where you can receive the wisdom you need to implement the lessons learned throughout the RoP and benefit from them for the rest of your life. As such you become a working example for others to follow.

Here are a few RoPs you may be able to relate to in one way or another. If you can recognise one or more of them it means you have passed through them.

A First RoP is that of a Catalyst. The first phase of separation begins when you become aware that you are psychic and you are drawn to use or develop your gifts. As you do so, you become a practising psychic and as such a catalyst for others and they for you. As already mentioned, this may result in friends, acquaintances and even close family members beginning to question your activities and a few may even distanc themselves from you (or vice versa).

As a consequence, the second phase, state of liminality, is taking place. In your reality, you are simply becoming who you are, and certainly not changing into somebody else.

As you self-empower, you enter the third phase, that of re-incorporation, where you function in your transformed state. This phase is also preparation for the first phase of the next RoP.

A Second RoP is that of Judgement and the limitations caused by being judgmental. By applying the three phases the issue of judgement of yourself during your spiritual awakening and empowerment, whilst not becoming judgmental of others, you can avoid limiting yourself whilst avoiding unnecessary learning curves.

One way of achieving this is by looking at a situation from the 'Little Picture' and the 'Big Picture', simultaneously.

- The Little Picture presents everyday events, the essential banal, the mundane and that which is akin to survival needs. Its spiritual function is to provide the questions and the challenges.

  We are in a position to make choices and experience the full consequences of those choices. Within the 'Little Picture' there are coincidences, failures, mistakes, rights and wrongs and judgment. They all create the essential learning curves and are accompanied by a relatively limited understanding as to the nature of 'why'.

- The Big Picture is the "eureka" moment. It is where we find the answers to the questions and solutions to the challenges held within the 'Little Picture'. The more we question and find solutions, the more our understanding and awareness as to the nature of 'why' develops and the better we are able to read the 'Big Picture'. The 'Big Picture' makes possible what is seen in the 'Little Picture' to be impossible.

  The 'Big Picture' provides additional dimensions that enable us to increase our understanding of the events that occur in the 'Little Picture'. It enables us to enter the realms of possibilities. As we do so we are given more choice.

As we learn to work with the 'Little' and 'Big Picture' in unison, where both concepts are used simultaneously, so we will create the medium sized picture, the middle path.

The middle path is where we have the best of both worlds. It is where harmony, peace and balance reside. It cannot exist without the Little and Big picture being in balance with each other. All this can be achieved by being non-judgemental whilst maintaining your judgement.

A Third RoP is that of Ego, which is a modified Id;without ego we have very little drive. If we feed our ego with success we stunt our personal and spiritual growth. By implementing the three phases to an understanding of what ego is can assist us in keeping it in check, whilst self-empowering and without annihilating the hard fought for personality.

Harnessing the ego enables us to recognise that those around us can be catalysts and by being so, help us become non-judgemental. Being non-judgemental enables us to understand and accept that we are all equal; no one is better or worse than another, we are simply different.

By applying the three phases; separation, the state of liminality and re-incorporation to the ego shows us that it is our differences that enable us to learn from each other, should be celebrated, not feared. Those who consider there is nothing to learn from another, regardless of who that 'another' is, appear to have have lost the plot, in fact they are onm a different path.

A Fourth RoP is that of Hypocrisy. It's another blind side that is rife within the human condition and we all suffer from it. It is a method we use to deceive ourselves first and by doing so we unwittingly deceive others.

We usually partake in this method of working out of the goodness of our hearts, which is why it is so difficult to identify. The sector of society that is most prone is the caring profession, and that includes practicing psychics. Our willingness to self-deceive knows no bounds, but the favourite method is to give advice to another, which will be sound, but not following it ourselves.

By applying the three phases to self empowerment we are able to reveal that which is being played out in the Big Picture. The next time you are moved to give advice to another, remember he or she will be reflecting back to you the same issue for you to deal with. If you respond with 'but I don't do that', you know you have hit the 'blindside' of hypocrisy.

A Fifth RoP is that of Self-empowerment and with it comes great responsibility. It takes humility to keep self-empowerment in check. The starting place for this concept is to understand that no one can help, harm or heal anyone but themselves. All three phases gives us an understanding of the following:

- Helping others: The need to help others comes from the fact we are all healers. For many the need to heal is so strong it is a vocation, for others it is a desire to help without thinking of the consequences to themselves or the person who they deem is in need of help. The fact is, we are all self-serving and we have to be to survive.

  From the 'Little Picture' it would appear these two human qualities are totally opposed but they are not. We have simply forgotten that if we cannot learn to help ourselves first, we cannot help another. It is only then by helping another, we help ourselves.

- Harming others: all those who are not self-empowered can cause harm by default and we are all disempowered until we start to self-empower. Harming another is the result of being hurt. Very few of us go out to deliberately harm another. Yet we all unwittingly hurt those around us, to a lesser or greater degree, every day. The more we hurt others the more we harm ourselves.
  Being harmed by another can only take place if we as adults allow it. If we allow it, we are in the process of balancing karma. The only way to reduce the incidences of being harmed and harming is to have one's personal

boundaries in place. Personal boundaries are not walls; they are the product of knowing when and how to assert in an appropriate manner.

NB Society is and has been built upon the male prerogative and privilege for millennia. It is a concept that imprisons both sexes resulting in neither knowing how or when to assert in a positive manner. This can only be balanced out by the emancipation of women, which started in the 1750s. When true equality is gained it will free both men and women.

- Healing others: We have been given certain tools to help us live our lives. The gift of healing is one of them. None of us have the ability to heal others, only Spirit can do that, through us.

Until the RoP of hypocrisy has been worked through, people forget they need to apply their healing gifts to themselves before they offer themselves to be used by Spirit to heal others. Never-the-less every time a person allows themselves to be used by Spirit to heal, they are also being healed themselves due to the issue of reflection.

Without introspection and dealing with who we are we cannot self-empower.

A Sixth RoP is that of Abusing Spirit. Abuse is another human trait and is learned behaviour. Most of us are blissfully ignorant to the fact that we are abusers, but most people consider that at some time in their lives they were abused whether it was mentally, emotionally or physically. One has to ask, if no one is the abuser, how is it we all feel abused at some stage in our lives? Applying the three phases; separation, the state of liminality and re-incorporation we can find an answer to this question. One has to ask, if no one is the abuser, how is it we can all feel and many are abused at some stage in our lives? Applying the three phases to the issue of abuse, we can find some of the answers to this complex question. One such answer is that although we are able to recognise physical or sexual abuse in others, most of us cannot identify what is mentally and emotionally abusive unless it is pointed out to us.

Whether we like it or not, we all knowingly or unknowingly abuse ourselves and by doing so, abuse others and therefore Spirit. We are abusing Spirit when we are:

- Not listening to those little messages we receive from Spirit, usually because we think we know better.
- Ignoring the co-incidences that we come across every day of our lives.
- Trying to speed up the process by ignoring the principle that everything has its own time.

A Seventh RoP is that of Respect. We cannot respect others if we do not respect ourselves first. When we disrespect others we disrespect ourselves. Applying the three phases; to the issue of respect shows that respecting another doesn't mean you have to agree with them, it is agreeing to disagree and allowing the differences to be, through compromise.

Self-respect is built on self-worth. Without self-worth we cannot recognise the gift that lies within us, which is ourselves.

The Self-made Traps

From the Big Picture, all Rites of Passage help us make the necessary self-made traps that enable us to create learning curves as well as to balance karma. They are essential components to self-empowerment and spiritual evolution.

Self-made traps are constructed in the sub-conscious and are all too easy to make and not that easy to get out of. Although traps limit freedom, in time they become safety zones from which a form of security is derived.

100

Releasing yourself from a self-made trap is achieved by accepting that your survival instincts dictate certain unpalatable behaviours, which result in self-sabotage. Once the type of self-sabotage is identified, the release trigger of the trap is activated. It is then up to the individual whether they temper their behaviour, thereby enabling them to leave the trap.

The release activates a learning curve, which when learnt, reveals an insight. The insight enables us not to unwittingly create and repeat an identical or similar learning curve.

Repeating similar learning curves is very easily done, since the 'variations on a theme' syndrome applies needs to be addressed before we truly learn.

17. Spiritual Journeys Can't Be Rushed?

Timing is another Rite of Passage; it is so precious it deserves its own chapter.

Some people come in with an innate understanding of Time at a subliminal level. Others find it elusive, an inconvenience or are scared of its passing. Time carries the one true certainty in every individual's life, physical death. Therefore it can be the greatest of healers and the wisest of all teachers on the earth plane, but only if we allow ourselves to move with the passing of time itself.

Time is relative, therefore an unexplained slowing down or speeding up can be experienced, depending upon the circumstances. As a result sometimes we may well feel that we are on a roller coaster. This is because we are.

Although time is subjective and doesn't exist in our minds, our hearts beat to it and our bodies are governed by the body clock. Only thought is not controlled by time but because our bodies are, it can often dictate when we think, what we think about timing and time itself.

A lot of energy is lost working against time and achieving very little as a result. By working with timeless energy is used and far more than what was thought possible can be achieved.

Working with Time and Delays
If you take the time to use time effectively it will be to your advantage. This advantage is an integral part of meeting goals and achieving.

Most of us can relate to going through one delay after another. Delays are usually caused by circumstances beyond our control. They cause us to become ungrounded through frustration and fear of missing something, e.g. a train, an item in a sale or an interview for a job, which ultimately leads to letting someone or ourselves down. All serious issues with serious consequences should we not be able to meet them.

All delays are Spirit's way of providing us with stop-gaps that can be used to review the situation in hand. By grounding you are taking the time to review a situation, therefore you have read the signs represented by the delay and by doing so have taken control of your life.

Reviewing a situation is never a waste of time, even if it confirms what is already known. It can provide a door-way opening to other possibilities that can only make themselves known during a review and when the time is right. As a consequence you are not a victim of circumstance but a survivor of it and therefore multi-tasking across the planes of existence.

Multi-tasking with Spirit

Multi-tasking is something we all do to a lesser or greater extent since it is a part of the human condition. Some people are naturally inclined toward multi-tasking and others are not.

All our physical and mental actions affect the other planes of our existence, which means that for every physical or mental action there are another six events that occur. Each event has a meaning and purpose, both of which cause reactions that ripple through the different dimensions. As a consequence all the other planes of existence are affected.

Multi-tasking enables a practising psychic to work in a measured, expansive, productive, balanced and harmonious way. It also enriches a spiritual journey, and as it does so, you become a person of depth. On a personal level, this depth will show itself in the relationship that you have with all those you know on the Earth plane and in Spirit.

An example of the spiritual multi-tasking can be given using a mediumship course. Tarot is a divination tool that complements mediumship. Adding the tarot cards keywords to the mediumship course module will only add a couple of minutes onto the studying time, which is achievable in anyone's schedule. The additional time compared to the additional information given and how it enriches the mediumship reading is incalculable.

The comparison between a mediumship reading with additional information derived from tarot and one without is palpable. It will have an in-depth and expansive quality about the reading that simply cannot exist otherwise. The student will also have an in-depth understanding of tarot thereby expanding his or her skill range, relatively effortlessly.

Because all divination tools correspond to each other, the temptation is to include numerology and astrology whilst working with the tarot. Before doing so bear in mind that it is important not to dilute the original course subject matter, which in this example is mediumship, thinking that it is being enriched.

The Spiritual Matrix

As you work time squared you automatically create the spiritual matrix, which enables access to the fourth dimension and beyond. Simultaneously working mentally, emotionally, spiritually and physically whilst interacting with Spirit, can lead you to use all your senses as a matter of course and without any effort.

As a consequence, you are receiving an abundance of information and knowledge, otherwise known as spiritual wealth. The process just described is a time-squared lifestyle known as working the, "Mind, Body Spirit, Work, Rest and Play Matrix".

Table VIII			
Spiritual Matrix			
	Mind	Body	Spirit
Work			
Rest			
Play			

You may think that the concept of multi-tasking directly opposes the statement 'spiritual journeys cannot be rushed'. This is not the case. All multi-tasking does is to show us just how much we can do in x amount of time in the time not normally used by the majority of us.

A Multi-tasking Lifestyle

Multi-tasking is not sustainable and can become both an obsession and therefore self-defeating. It takes discipline and organisation because time can easily run away with itself and take the psychic with it, irrespective of how skilled they are.

Such a lifestyle is very productive if managed. Using the spiritual matrix enables a situation to be identified, considered and simultaneously analyzed from different viewpoints. It also encourages tolerance and counteracts dogma. This means you are not constrained by linear thinking and start to work with non-linear thought, allowing inspired creativity to filter through.

A multi-tasking lifestyle can empower the individual spiritually as well as emotionally, mentally and physically. As a consequence the processes of transformation, re-birthing or metamorphosis take place and with it comes the grey zone.

The Grey Zone

Multi-tasking when appropriate enables us to see what it is that we need, rather than what we want. This realisation represents another door-way, which leads into working within the grey zone, where nothing is as simple as it originally appears in the black and white zones.

From the metaphysical perspective, the grey zone can be associated with the subconscious, the subliminal and where past life influences are at their most powerful, the domain of Spirit.

When functioning in the grey zone the ability to see beyond what is obvious comes to the fore. This enables the detection of and ability to witness the workings beneath the surface and how what is upon the surface manifests. In other words you can read what is hidden, or not. The choice is yours.

The grey zone can be a confusing place if you remain in it too long and do not use common sense whilst working with what is being revealed. It is important to remember why you entered the grey zone in the first place, otherwise the whole process becomes self-defeating.

18. "Spirit Helps Those Who Help Themselves"

Spirit lies within; it is there to support during decision-making. It cannot make independent decisions upon a person's behalf nor is it responsible for a person's actions or reactions to a given circumstance or event. Spirit can only assist when a person chooses to help him or herself. The sanctity of free will demands that this is so.

Free will rules, even if the pull to follow Spirit may be so strong that it feels there is no choice but to follow it. Follow Spirit yes, but to do so blindly indicates a person is in the process of avoiding taking responsibility for his or herself. They are not helping themselves and it may well cost them dearly. Remember it is Spirit that can survive without food and shelter - we cannot.

Those who follow Spirit without using their intelligence and rationale are going though the heavy learning curve of trusting too much in Spirit and not enough in themselves. As a consequence they are unwittingly looking for trade-offs.

Trade-offs Don't Apply

A trade-off is a valid way of working within the orthodox world and we are all prone to making and benefiting from them. Trade-offs with Spirit are not appropriate. This is because we have nothing to trade.

Therefore working with Spirit doesn't guarantee financial success, as some people think or expect it to be.

The commonest trade-off is the concept that a person will receive three-fold back in turn for what they give. The fact is from a personal and spiritual perspective of wealth we get back far more than that. When it is applied to financial gain and taken literally this concept wreaks havoc.

The Great Escape

Most trade-offs centre round making life easier or escaping it altogether - without dying that is.

The pull to escape the monotony, trials and tribulations of our lives is always present and many of us are looking for a 'get out' clause without realising. When a spiritual high presents such a clause, for some the temptation to enter a state of giddy abandonment is impossible to resist.

From the 'Little Picture', it appears that those who simply get up and go have literally lost their senses. And from that perspective they have but not from the 'Big Picture'. From there, such people have felt a spiritual high, have chosen not to be grounded and are therefore out of their rationale. It is the place where they need to be in order to balance karma and go through a learning curve associated with avoidance and self-responsibility.

It takes great courage for a person to walk these paths and greater courage to put the learning curve into practice rather than beating themselves up once they become grounded again.

Balancing Karma whilst Going Through Learning Curves

The pull of Spirit cannot be underestimated. It is an integral part of the process to balance karma and go through learning curves. The learning curves are played out during the process of the balancing of karma.

At this stage in our spiritual evolvement, we have to come out of our rationale to balance karma. The issue is the further out we go the higher the risk of creating new karma, whilst achieving the original goal. We can lower this risk by maintaining some degree of grounding whilst going through this process.

In time it is possible to identify when a balancing of karma and learning curve are coming into being before they happen. It is then we are able to approach the situation with knowledge and understanding rather than ignorance and unawareness.

At this point we are aware of the consequences of our own actions before we act, we have balanced karma mentally and do not have to go through the process physically. This is the power of Free Will.

So although spiritual journeys cannot be rushed, and we cannot expect Spirit to do all the work, there is still freedom of choice to choose which route we can take, the longer or the shorter way. NB The shorter way isn't necessarily the quicker nor the easier way.

19. Walk Your Talk as a Practising Psychic

Spiritual reality runs parallel to our materialised reality. Our materialised reality is made up of a succession of creating and balancing karma, going through learning curves and benefiting accordingly.

Both realities are inevitably linked and are perceived differently by all of us. Practising psychics are able to read both these realities concurrently and by doing so are able to embrace the complexities of both realities separately as well as combined.

An understanding of how both realities are interlinked is important if a psychic wishes to take full responsibility for the ramifications of possessing and developing such a gift.

Materialized Reality

In keeping with the principles of metaphysics, we are what we think - such is the power of the mind that thought in all forms, whether daydreaming, conscious, or sub-conscious, creates reality. In order for us to bring our thoughts into being, we need intention and then action.

Understanding this is the key to realising that we can all change our individual realities and therefore our social environments for the better without compromising our true selves.

The social environment within which we live is a result of our own individual actions or inaction. When - as individuals - we work to change our individual realities for the greater good, we also improve the social environment within which we live - without affecting our own or another's free will. The difference is palpable. Therefore our perception of reality is based on our upbringing, which is in turn influenced by culture, the environment, education, values and inherent genes.

Spiritual Reality

Spiritual reality is a limitless, timeless and matter-less environment within which there are no restrictions. If anyone perceives there are limitations within spiritual reality it is because that person has placed them there.

Spiritual reality is a place where anything can happen and all things are possible. It is this place that our dreams and aspirations come from. Spirit works with the concept of intention, before action and reaction have taken place, as well as after it. Therefore spiritual reality is a very different reality to that of materialised reality.

Spiritual reality lies within as well as surrounding. The upshot of this is our intentions are far more significant than we realise. Irrespective of whether or not we follow through upon our intention on the earth plane, it is carried out within the etherics at the time of the thought.

The Role of Intention

Intention is complex. It plays an integral role within the subconscious, thought and the mind since it is one of the cornerstones of creation. There is an intention for every thought, least of all action since without intention there can be no manifestation.

From the metaphysical viewpoint intention also plays a major role in manifestation since it is the bedrock of magik.

From a spiritual viewpoint there are three levels of intention, the Shadow level, the Soul level and the Conscious level. They enable us to have the ability to create our desires, but only when we have understood that we rarely get what we want, we usually get what we need. Once we are aware of our desires, all three levels are unified and manifestation can take place.

This much we know, what is open to question is what happens to intentions that do not manifest. One concept is that they become disembodied thoughts that manifest alternate realities. From the 'big picture', this means there is no such thing as an intention that does not manifest in one form or another.

For the practising psychic, intention is a tool that can be used to enable a person to change their reality. Therefore it is important to have a basic understanding of the role intention has within the earth plane and how Spirit plays an integral part in its purpose:

A person intends to cut down a tree.

The split second that person conceives that thought, the Tree Spirit vacates the tree.

The physical tree is left in a form of suspended animation, living but without its Spirit.

If the person carries out his or her intention, the Tree Spirit returns to its natural Light-being state.

If the person doesn't carry out his or her intention, the Tree Spirit returns to take up residence in the tree it left.

The unrealised intention goes on to materialise a reality where the tree was cut down.

The nature of the intention as to whether it is positive or challenging, can manifest in the concept of right and wrong.

The Concept of Right and Wrong

Most of us believe we have a pretty good sense of what is 'right' and 'wrong'. This sense is based on the guidelines of the spiritual beliefs of a culture and the Laws of the Country. Just a couple of examples of this are Ten Commandments in the Old Testament or the Koran. Their style of language may be outdated now, but the fundamental principles are not.

What isn't often taken into account with regard to what is deemed right and wrong is an individual's interpretation and personal justification. As the Most Rev. Dr Desmond Tutu said, we are all made for goodness. Even so both of these issues can take us into the grey areas of both morals and ethics.

These grey areas are governed by what a person thinks is right at the time and his or her conscience. This concept could be considered to be another corner stone of metaphysics.

Practising and professional psychics need to be aware that everyone has different values and those values need to be respected, even if those values are alien to their own value system, since this is why grey areas exist. It is therefore essential to have both a moral and ethical premise to work from, which also falls within the laws governing the profession.

Here are some guidelines to consider when working as a professional psychic or a practicing one:

- Avoid predicting.
- Try not to transfer your issues onto the client/friend.
- Avoid relaying what you know the client wants to hear instead of keeping quiet or tell what you are receiving.
- Avoid making judgements by telling someone they are wrong and you are right.
- Avoid telling a client/friend there is negativity or evil around them.
- Avoid taking it personally when someone doesn't accept a message.

Spiritual Possession

When a psychic begins working with Spirit, it can appear to the on-looker that Spirit is taking possession of the psychic. This is not the case.

Spiritual possession is an excellent example of a fear-based concept that has snowballed out of control to manifest something that it isn't and by doing so is masking the true nature of the event. Thus a grey area is formed.

The true nature of such events is that a psychic is agreeing to and thereby giving permission for Spirit to work through him or her in specific ways. These ways are known as mental mediumship, telekinesis and telepathy, trance work and channeling.

This way of working is known as a spiritual partnership.

Spiritual Partnerships

When a psychic partners Spirit, they become united in a manner that is impossible with any other type of spiritual work. Although the partnership is temporary, Spirit manifests in a particularly powerful manner and it changes the behavior of the person.

Spiritual partnering is an ancient practice and we have all inherited the ability to do so. It is a very natural, harmless and enriching activity and is essential to our general well being. To this very day, there are many tribal communities that perform rituals based on this procedure as a part of their culture. There are those known as, 'carers', usually older members of the community who no longer partake in the practice themselves, and they oversee these rituals. As a consequence, mental mediumship or the possession of a person by a Spirit is seen as a positive event and one that benefits the community as a whole.

When Spirit separates from the person, the partnership is over and so too is the spiritual experience. The person is celebrated, respected and looked after until they are sufficiently grounded.

These rituals do not cause any mental trauma because they are an integral part of the tribe's way of living.

In western culture, often the psychic medium is taken unawares by the process of partnering with Spirit and may very well have no memory after the event. This is understandable. To those who don't understand, it may appear that the person has been possessed, so from their perspective possession has taken place and harm has been caused, despite the fact that this is not necessarily the case.

The Fear of Demonic Possession

It is an archaic belief that has no role in a modern society, yet demonic possession is the mainstay of the majority of mainstream religions. It is a concept borne out of ignorance and it disempowers individuals by feeding their innermost fears - that which is created by fear itself and what some call the devil. And it does so very effectively.

What is perceived to be demonic possession is in fact an unaware, psychically active person who is not in control of his or her gifts and has become deranged. The Id is fed by fear of the situation and insanity occurs when the Id is out of control.

Fear of the unknown can drive a person into hysteria, as can a substance or a medical condition. Therefore a doctor, a professional psychic whose expertise is within this field and/or a psychiatrist should be called to assist.

The fact of the matter is that no guide, Angel or loved one is powerful enough to force a person to act as a channel against his or her will. We would live in a very different world if that were the case.

Mental Illness

As already mentioned, the correlations being drawn between mental illness and the psychic are due, in part, to the medical profession not embracing that our psychic ability is an intrinsic aspect of our spirituality.

Mental illness can and does occur, it is part of the human condition. We all suffer from one form or another of mental illness throughout our lives. It is one of the symptoms caused by living in a fear driven society.

Therefore most people do not mention that they have witnessed or undergone a psychic phenomenon - why? Because they are scared that they or someone else will think they are going mad.

The few who do consult a doctor run the very real risk of being diagnosed as suffering from a mental condition, which can range from being depressed, suffering from multi-personality disorder to schizophrenia, to name but a few.

From a metaphysical perspective all such conditions are associated with personal and spiritual evolvement, as the examples given show:

- Depression is a natural condition produced by the mind to show the person a change in their lifestyle is needed. If the change doesn't take place, then clinical depression usually develops.

- Multi-personality disorder is dimension hopping and begins when a person remembers his or her past lives or their activities in parallel existences. Usually what triggers this memory is abuse in some form or another. The abuse will be associated with the person balancing karma and the different personalities provide a coping mechanism.

- Schizophrenia, the origin of which is when a person begins to interact with the archetypes through his or her clairaudient abilities.

usually by the time diagnosis is made it is often too late to deal with such issues purely from the psychic perspective. Therefore medical intervention and treatment is essential. If part of that treatment could involve psychic expertise, it would help a lot of sufferers, but only those who are mentally fit to be able to process such information

It is no co-incidence that there is a percentage of patients in mental hospitals who think they are angels, E.Ts., Merlin or Napoleon. This is because there is an aspect of him or her self who is. They have not been trained to deal with this aspect and are therefore unable to manage the experiences they under-go, and it screws their heads up.

If caught in time and if such people were taught how to harness their gifts, many of their 'symptoms' would, in time, dissipate. It is devastating for the person who is incorrectly diagnosed.

The psychological reaction to an incorrect diagnosis is the same as that of a curse. That reaction opens the gates to the self-fulfilling prophecy syndrome. In other words, the person who is psychic and has been told they are mentally ill, may well become become ill, despite the fact they are not, they are psychic.

Obviously, the blessing of a diagnosis is when it is correct and it means the person can start the healing process.

20. Dreams, Correspondences, Symbolism, Signs, Elements, the Elementals and Divination

In order to give an enriched informative reading, a psychic needs to have an understanding of the methods Spirit uses to deliver the information. Divination tools are these methods. They enable psychics to detect, contact and communicate with what can be found in the etherics.

What is found in the etherics are our archetypes, guides, angels, loved ones and the Elementals, to name but a few. The messages they have for us are interpreted using dreams, symbols, the elements, and the ability to decode this elusive world using correspondences. This relaying of messages makes us a part of the hyper-communication network.

Dreams

'Oneiromancy', or dream interpretation is a source of both information and inspiration and is used for divination purposes. Dreams can take a major role in any psychic reading since dreams are the key to the subconscious and pre-subconscious.

From the metaphysical perspective, dreams are what we do in another reality, and some think it is where, as humans, we do our most important work.

Dreams usually use symbolism in one form or another, and

need to be interpreted. Even the dreams where you think the messages are obvious still need investigating.

How and why we dream isn't fully understood but what is known is that dreaming has a function, it helps us process what we cannot first fully comprehend and is also a form of stress release. The scarier the dream the more stress is released.

The majority of people dream in total for approximately 2 hours a night. Rapid eye movement (REM) indicates when a person is dreaming, but it has been known for people to dream in a non REM (NREM) state. From a psychic's viewpoint, REM occurs when we retrieve, receive and process information whether it is during sleep or a meditation.

There are various forms of dreaming, including lucid, light, normal and deep dreams. Lucid dreaming is when one is conscious whilst in a dream state and therefore has control of the details of the dream itself. It is used in directed meditations and has been scientifically verified.

Dreams of absent-minded transgression (DAMT) are when the dreamer absent-mindedly performs an action that he or she has been trying to stop. Examples of this are a recovering alcoholic having drinking dreams or an ex-smoker dreaming of lighting up a cigarette, or a student dreaming they have failed their exam only to wake finding that they haven't even taken the exam.

These dreams can be so real that the dreamer awakes thinking that actually happened and feeling guilty. It has been shown that DAMT plays a positive part in ensuring the dreamer meets his or her goal.

From the metaphysical perspective, the dream world lies within the dimensions and inter-dimensions as well as within the ethereal plane. Dream world is the domain of all the different facets of Spirit, alternative and parallel realities and what is hidden.

One line of thought considers that our true work is done within the dream world. If this is correct, our conscious state is merely there to sustain our physical bodies for when we enter dream state to do our work.

Another concept considers that the reality we live in is nothing but a dream created by our Collective State and brought about by the power of the mind to form matter.

Correspondences, Signs and Symbolism

The majority of messages received from Spirit are in code and need to be decoded. Correspondences, synergy, co-incidences, signs and symbols are the keys used to decipher these codes. They are the tools used by Spirit to help us understand how the Collective exists, how it works and the role we have to play within it. They have been used since before the advent of the alphabet, which are themselves made up of symbols and signs.

As already mentioned, correspondences arise when two or more different or similar and unassociated items infer the same thing.

Symbolism is the ancient practice of applying symbolic meanings to objects, events, and relationships; this also covers the relationship you have with yourself and others.

Signs, another ancient practice, are something that means something to someone in some way.

The four cornerstones of divination are scrying, tarot, astrology and numerology, each of which are made up of signs and symbols. Using them individually or combined, they can reveal what is hidden, and that is the true meaning of a dream or whatever is happening in 'awake' time. It really is as simple as that. Using Tarot, as an example, works as shown in the flow chart opposite.

By using the keywords from astrology, tarot, colour and numerology and applying them to the correspondences you will be able to decode any message from Spirit. It is a very simple way of working with a very complex issue. With experience and time you will be decoding messages from Spirit without thinking about it.

There are always exceptions to a rule, and the exception to

120

The symbolism on the tarot card release the information to your higher self

which comes through to your conscious self

which is applied to the reading and forms a message

which corresponds to and symbolizes the client

who is in turn represented by the correspondences and symbolism on the tarot card

this one is: do not take any message from Spirit at face value. Never forget, Spirit works hidden. The messages that appear to be straightforward need to be decoded in the same manner as those that don't make sense immediately.

Reading the Correspondences, Signs and Symbols

Psychics retrieve information from Spirit by reading the signs and symbols. Both are also tools of divination in their own right, as well as playing an integral part in reading correspondences. So too is what is happening within the environment of the reading that is taking place. A few examples are as follows:

- If the client's doorbell goes in a middle of a reading, it means the client needs to stop and have time to assimilate and probably look at the information from a different perspective. This assimilation takes place whilst the client is opening the door and dealing with the situation in hand.

- If a butterfly is seen in the garden during a reading, it means transformation is necessary or is taking place.

- If an owl is heard, wisdom is needed.

Again, the list is endless.

Omens and Auguries

These entities fall under the heading of symbolism. There seems to be some confusion with regard to the role of omens, which have a bad press, as too with auguries. Both are signs giving advanced warning of a positive or challenging event. They are usually read through the events of nature. A famous omen is depicted in Shakespeare's Julius Caesar, 'Beware the ides of March', which referred to the 15th day in March, the day Caesar was assassinated.

Correspondences in Action

Correspondences bring to the surface the continuous contact that we enjoy with Spirit on a subliminal level. They are a very effective way of identifying individual messages being received from Spirit and providing confirmation of other messages as well. They can also act as a guide; follow the trail they leave and you can find answers in any given circumstance and can benefit accordingly. There will come a time when the process becomes unproductive and when you reach this place it is time to stop. You will be in possession of the information you need.

There are also biological and associative correspondences and it is essential to have a basic understanding of these two areas if you wish to provide an in-depth as well as an enhanced reading.

- Examples of just a few biological correspondences are: -
  o The head is associated with the sun

- o The throat is associated with blue for communication
- o The kidneys are associated with water, emotions, love
- o Legs are associated with moving.
- o The spine is associated with structure.
- o Expelling bodily wastes, coughing, sneezing = detoxing
- o A broken leg = someone is being forced to stop and re-assess
- o Lungs = pride

- Examples of associative correspondences are: -
  - o 100 translates as 10 or 1 = concept of new beginnings, Aries
  - o Scorpio = female, blue-green/turquoise, Uranus
  - o Red = sex, danger, assertion, anger, power
  - o High = bright and light
  - o Low = dark and heavy
  - o Even = solutions, easier times
  - o Uneven = problems, difficult times
  - o Square = solid, stuck
  - o Circle = curves, circling, completion, unknown beginning and end, female
  - o Triangle = hierarchy, three in one mystery, male

These few examples show that the messages from Spirit are constant and if we have the desire to read them we can benefit accordingly.

Keywords in Relation to Correspondences

We have already focused a lot on keywords and this in itself highlights the importance of their role when working with Spirit. Using tarot as an example, here is a working example of how keywords and correspondences work together:

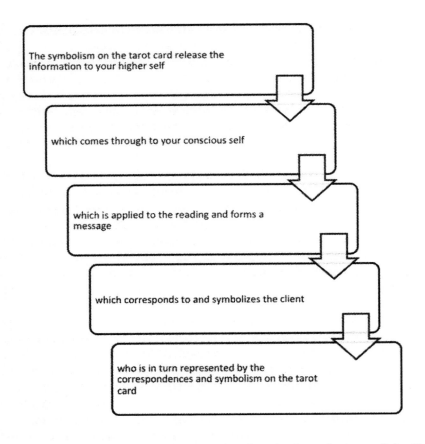

As you will see, the process is identical to that used in the symbolism tarot flow chart. Again, the messages from Spirit are hidden, but only in plain sight. As such they are available to anyone who cares to take the time and effort to use the keywords and notice the correspondences

The Elements and Elementals
Earth, air, fire, water and ether are five elements of Mother Nature and help form the bedrock of metaphysics and alchemy. The elements also gave birth to the periodic table of

elements in chemistry and are applied to engineering, physics and biology,

The elements are the building blocks of all life forms and as such are one of the components that enable the concept of correspondences to exist.

With the exception of ether, any of these elements can enhance or extinguish the others. By doing so they create another state of existence. Examples of this are:

• Water can control or quench fire, flood or feed the earth and consume or cleanse the air.
• Fire can warm or boil water until it turns into steam, scorch or warm the earth, consume or warm the air.
• Air can bring life to fire or disperse it, bring life to or erode the earth, oxygenate or suffocate water.
• Earth can enable life or destroy it by employing, air, fire and water.

And then there is the Fifth Element, which represents all things quantum, ethereal, unworldly - the world of Spirit, which exists within each one of the elements.

All five elements are represented by Elementals, beings that are attuned to, or are composed of, the element itself. Elementals make themselves known to us through the elements they represent. Reference to the Elementals was first found in the alchemical works of Paracelsus and are as follows:

Table IX		
The Five Elementals		
Name	Latin	Element
Sylph	Sylvestris	Air
Pygmy	Gnomus (gnome)	Earth
Salamander	Vulcanus	Fire
Nymph	Undina (undine)	Water
The 5th Element	Quintessence	Ether

However they were well established in folklore and mythology long before Paracelsus.

The function of the Elementals is to assist us to work with the element they represent. Their activity is often witnessed on the mundane physical level, the most obvious being the weather and the effect it has upon the earth. From a metaphysical perspective, the Elementals are not to be messed with. Look at the energy it takes to produce a hurricane, tsunami, a volcanic eruption or forest fire and you will understand why.

Being active within the etherics means we automatically connect to the elements and therefore the Elementals. Therefore we are well practiced in raising the Elementals whether we realise it or not. As we work with elements, the Elementals make themselves known to us. It won't be surprising to read that anything can be used as a divination tool, including our fingers. The thumb represents ether; the forefinger, earth; the middle finger water; the ring finger the air; and the little finger fire. Whether you know it or not, every time you point at someone using your forefinger you raise Pygmy. Therefore, everything either represents the Elementals, or corresponds – directly or indirectly – to them.

Whether you know it or not, every time you point at someone using the forefinger you raise Pygmy

Speaking or thinking the words of earth, air, fire, water and ether will raise the Elementals irrespective of the context. Activating the Elementals is another matter.

Raising doesn't mean activating. You can raise an Elemental through everyday conversation but to activate an Elemental you need to have the knowledge to do so. This knowledge also comes within the realms of magik. Here are some examples of everyday living activities through which we raise the Elementals:-

• By striking a match or lighting a lighter, you are raising Salamander.

• When running a tap you are raising Nymph.

• Spending or receiving money raises Pygmy.

• With each breath you raise Sylph.

• Working Spirit whether through prayer or psychic activity in one form or another you raise the 5th Element – Divinity.

The elementals are also raised through symbols and signs, which are to be found on some tarot decks, wands, symbolic jewellery and in many designs. Below are the symbols that represent the elements in tarot.

Table X The Elements and Tarot				
Earth	Air	Fire	Water	Ether
Pygmy	Sylph	Salamander	Nymph	The 5th Element
Disks	Swords	Wands	Cups	Major Arcana

21. Tools of the Trade

Every profession has its tools to do the job. Although psychics themselves are the tools for their job, most possess one or more sacred items, which can also be used as divination tools.

Divination tools act as an agent between the psychic and Spirit and as such are sacred. Those who do not use them are no better than the psychics who do - it is a matter of choice. If you are not drawn to have any such item when working, please do not think you have to force yourself to find something.

Sacred items can range from angel ornaments and dream catchers to lucky charms, or jewellery worn or placed by the psychic as he or she works. Here are some of the more recognisable divination tools:

Crystals, Tarot, Angel cards, a stone tied to the end of a piece of string – a pendulum, the I Ching, tea leaves, crystal balls, water, black ink, astrology, flowers, tree parts such as branches suitable for dowsing or divining rods, runes and various parts of dead wildlife.

Quantity Doesn t Equate to Quality

Understand this. A £1 tumble stone/crystal will be just as powerful as something that costs £100 and is ten times the size of the same mineral. One pack of tarot is no better or worse than another, just different. A second hand pack of tarot is just as good as a new one. A straight wooden stick found in a forest is just as powerful as a crafted wand. A small marble is as powerful as a crystal ball.

Your Choice?

When exercising your free will to become a practising psychic you give permission to all that is within the etherics to work with you. Therefore, for those who wish to work with divination tools, you choosing it is not an option. It chooses you and you are led by it to where it is. This applies whether you are given a pack of tarot or a crystal etc. Whether you accept this to be the case is another matter.

If you find yourself being drawn into a shop, make a note of what jumps out at you. Being inexplicably drawn to something that does not fall within your present modus operandi means Spirit is at work. At such times, be sure to use your common sense when following the signs – especially where money is concerned. By doing so, you will end up with what you need when you need it, whilst also showing respect to the money Deities.

If a delay is experienced, such as a shop being closed or for some reason or they have run out of stock, it will be because you are working with timing. Therefore, employ the timing guidelines since Spirit is testing you – as it does at times.

Once you have your divination tool, or rather it has you, don't expect miracles to happen. Although the connection is instantaneous at the time of intent, you may not feel a physical, emotional or mental connection and you may feel the spiritual connection wane.

At this point do not fall into the temptation of thinking "It doesn't work" and buying something else or giving up. You need to learn how to work with your agent and it needs to learn how to work with you. This process is called bonding. This bonding incorporates all the person's psychic abilities.

You and Your Divination Tool

Forming a conscious bond with your agent may be immediate or it may take time. If it takes time - as with all bonding processes - it will take interaction, and this is done through commitment and practice. Put the item to one side and try again the next day. When an instant bonding occurs that meets your every expectation it usually means you have worked in the same field with the same or similar item in a past life, and the memories are flooding back. Such reactions are not sustainable and you may find the next time you pick it up, with the expectation of a similar response, that you receive nothing.

This is normal and you simply start the process of bonding with your tools in this lifetime.

There are psychics who genuinely think they cannot function without their divination tool. When this occurs, it can be due to the psychic having transferred his or her natural abilities onto the agent. As a consequence, he or she has lost confidence in their own abilities to function without the item, whether it takes the form of a necklace, wand, tarot cards or lucky charm. This lack of confidence develops an over-dependency upon the divination tool rather than the agent aspect of the tool.

Alternatively, the agent and psychic may have bonded to such an extent that they have become one and there are no over-dependency issues to deal with.

The Sacredness of it All

The tools of this trade, irrespective of what they are, are considered sacred since they all have their own spiritual energy, function and purpose. As agents their function is to enhance the work of a psychic. The agent transmits information through itself, which is forged by its spiritual energy and purpose. Therefore all such items need to be given the respect and recognition that is due to them.

A psychic's gift is to receive the information transmitted through the tool and make sense of it. Thus the communication loop is formed.

The Communication Loop

As long as the communication loop is active, you are functioning as a practising psychic. This process occurs irrespective of the methodology used, i.e. Mediumship, clairvoyance, clairaudience, clairsentience etc., and with or without divination tools.

This loop develops automatically as you work with Spirit, so you do not have to think or worry about it. For those who use an agent the following process takes place when divining.

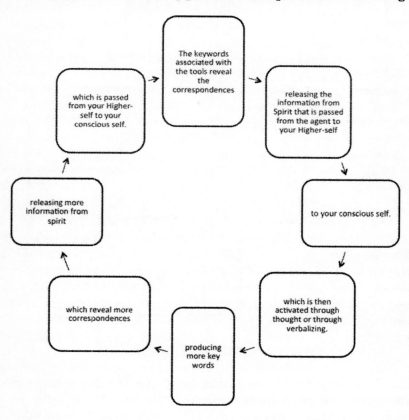

The communication loop works in a similar way for those who do not use an agent. The difference lies in that the information does not have the input of the tool itself. Instead it connects directly with the psychic.

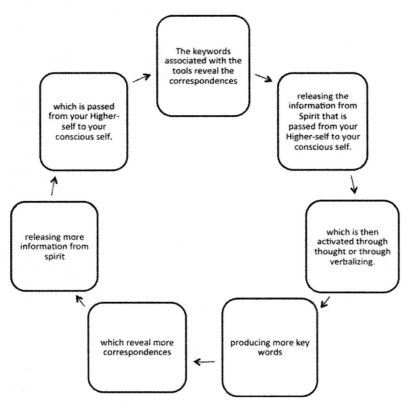

The loop itself forms the structure of the reading while the keywords and correspondences provide the information in language format. The structure of the language dictates your method of working which will be unique to the psychic.

Superstition

Superstition runs deep in everyone's psyche and it is a learning curve that we all work with and go through. Superstition can be seen as the collective memories of the past and is associated with less enlightened times. From a metaphysical perspective, those who are superstitious are showing they are subliminally aware of past lives when they were victims of superstition.

Being superstitious produces a self-fulfilling prophecy where you think something bad will happen and it does. This is not because you didn't have your divination tool or lucky charm with you, but because you approached a situation with a fear-based attitude which undermined your abilities.

Whenever something is considered sacred, superstition usually accompanies it. Examples are "it is bad luck to use divination tools to read for yourself". Another superstition is that that 'no good' will come if a ritual isn't first performed before working with Spirit.

If someone tells you it's "good" or "bad luck" to do or not to do something, I strongly suggest you ignore them. At the end of the day, respecting yourself is all that is necessary to respect your craft. Learning self-respect occurs naturally once you start to take control of your life.

Luck

There is no doubt luck exists, it has at least three formats: luck that is derived from a positive personality and luck that occurs by 'chance'. The third is also associated when our Higher-self wishes to provide us with a gift.

Being alchemic in nature, luck by 'chance' is what happens when we wittingly or unwittingly connect to the flow of life. Lucky charms and spells are one way of connecting to this flow but everything is relative. They cannot change a person's luck, if what is actually happening is that he or she is going through a process of balancing karma and a learning curve. Such times are called ebbing times. However they dp provide support for those who beleive in them, and on occasion have saved lives. That is no mean feat.

There is no doubt that metaphysics can assist a person by helping them work through the ebbing times, rather than giving up. Rituals, divination tools and/or luck charms provide a structure that can do this. But at the end of the day it is the person who possesses the power to change their 'luck' for better or worse.

22. Unlocking the door of Knowledge

Once in possession of the keys of correspondence, the symbols and signs etc., you are in a position to consider answering some of life's questions. What may appear to be something trivial to one person will not be so to another. Some issues are banal, others are not and all have relevance and therefore need to be answered one way or another. Fundamentally we all wish to know the following:

- Why am I here?

- Where have I come from?

- Where am I now?

- Where am I going?

- What am I doing?

- Why am I doing it?

- What options are available?

- What should I do first, second, third, and so on to identify or get closer to my goals?

- What is going to happen to me?

- Why did that happen?

- Why me?

The Mother of all Questions is WHEN?

The role of the practicing and professional psychic is to act as a channel and relay information from Spirit to the client. During this process a client will want to know what will happen and when. It is not the place of the psychic to either provide the client with a definitive answer or to predict. If delivered in a responsible and practical manner, the information enables the client to find the answers to their questions.

The Art of Prediction

A prediction is giving a client a date and/or time of an event in the future. All psychics have the ability to predict but they cannot guarantee the occurrence. This is because no psychic knows categorically where the information they are receiving comes from; whether it is a past, present, future or parallel life of the client, and all of which have their own past and future and parallels existences which the client is also active within.

Each one of these existences has a timeline. The information received from Spirit will be valid and correct but not applicable if it is applied to an inappropriate timeline.

If a practicing or professional psychic gives an inappropriate timeline, he or she can unwittingly ruin a person's life. Furthermore, people's lives have been ruined because clients have believed in a prediction only for the event to not materialise.

The Fraudulent Mediums Act 1951 was repealed in April 2007 due to an EU directive and replaced by the Consumer Protection from Unfair Trading 2007. This means that, in the UK, it is now against the law to predict. As a result a client can sue a psychic, if he or she predicts and that prediction doesn't come to pass in the timeline stated or inferred.

Despite this change in the law, a substantial number of people still go to a psychic for predictions. By doing so they are, by default, asking the psychic to break the law.

Such people are either vulnerable, do not understand the ramifications of asking for a prediction or they do not know the law has changed. It is up to the psychic to tell them without losing clients. There are subtle ways of getting the message across, even before the client has contacted you:

- If a professional psychic, look to the wording on your advert and/or website and do not use any phrases or words that state you predict.

- Include in your introduction before a reading that you do not predict.

- Put the information that you receive from Spirit and you know to be so in a non-predictive manner using open-ended phraseology.

- Provide your client with choice; there are always two or more paths in approaching any situation. Give more than one path; allow them to choose which path they need to take.

- If after you have explained that it is against the law to predict, and your client still presses for a prediction, you must refuse to give a specific timeline. A vague near or distant future will suffice, however the best response is "If you need this to happen you need to make it happen, when are you going to start to act and make it happen?"

Timelines

For those who haven't heard of the word, a timeline is a sequence of events that take place over a period of time. Without a timeline, prediction cannot take place.

Divining is based on timelines because this practice uses the sum total of our existence. This includes the past, present and future and the parallel lifetimes and parallel existences, as mentioned earlier. Even if the issue of reincarnation is taken out of the equation the psychic still has to contend with the timelines of the present lifetime and its various options.

If a psychic doesn't take the timeline of a client's existence into consideration at the time of doing the reading, he or she may find they give a very shallow reading or one that simply doesn't make sense to the client.

It is possible to use timelines and not predict. This is done by not being specific when it comes to dates. If information is being given from Spirit, it needs to be made clear at the time that it could be from a past, parallel or future lifetime.

The client will be able to make sense of it when presented in the format that they are in the process of balancing karma from a past lifetime, whilst going through learning curves in the present lifetime.

Always remember that the information you provide as a reading can influence the decision making of a client. This means that the choices made in the present can affect the future, as past actions affect the present.

Take responsibility for your role in this scenario and in time it will enable you to provide an enriched and meaningful reading that enables the client to provide him or herself with the answers, rather than thinking they need to look to another. This is only possible when the information is not given in a predictive manner.

23. Experience is the Ultimate Teacher

Ask yourself this: as a client, who you would choose, a qualified psychic with no experience, or an experienced psychic with no qualifications? You need to bear your answer in mind when deciding to develop your gifts to the level where you become a practising or professional psychic.

Practice is what turns gifts into abilities and abilities into a skill. Whether a psychic is naturally academic or intuitive is irrelevant at this stage. What is important is that you approach the issue with an open mind and no preconceived expectations.

The decision as to whether to go on a course is very simple if based upon finances. If you can't afford to go on a course, you teach yourself (DIY).

If you do have the finances to spare, you will want a good return on your investment. Therefore the decision needs to be based upon which way is best for you.

If you are not academic, do not allow what may have been negative school experiences to stop you from considering attending a course, but consider going on a weekend workshop first, just to see how you get on. It is important to bear in mind that adults attending courses are taught very differently to children at school. Furthermore, any course worth its salt will have ways and means of assisting those who have learning difficulties.

If you are academic, do not expect the courses to be run on the same exacting academic standards you may be used to.

The Pros and Cons of Psychic Courses and Workshops

There are courses and workshops that will cater for both academic and intuitive psychics. It will depend upon the curriculum and structure as to whether a course will help or hinder.

There are so many psychic courses that to the novice it can be quite bewildering. Too much choice can lead to no choice being made. When making enquiries, consider discounting those that don't fit easily into your present lifestyle. However, your decisions must ultimately be based upon whether you need to have recognised and accredited qualifications. If you are not sure as to which topic you wish to take, first opt for a weekend workshop so you can make an informed decision. Also bear in mind that intensive weekend courses can be just as effective as a 'one day a week for three months' course.

Another way of deciding how to develop your psychic abilities is to choose whether you wish to use a divination tool, or not. If you do, decide which divination tool you feel most comfortable with and then look at the different types of course that fall within that field. Tarot uses all the psychic senses so it is a value for money course.

No one can teach you how to become a psychic because you already are one. Those that hold courses can only facilitate in the process. Their primary function is to create an environment, which enables a person to identify and develop their gifts, not to become skilled. That takes practice.

If someone claims to be able to teach you, for argument's sake, tarot, what they are actually saying is that they can teach you the theory of it. You already possess the gift to read tarot, which is why you chose the course in the first place. You will discover your individual reading technique whilst attending the course.

The College of Psychic Studies[7] is a good place to start making enquiries. Their website provides a mass of information that you can use to help you decide which area you wish to develop first; e.g., mediumship, clairvoyance,

140

clairaudience, clairsentience, remote viewing etc. Then find a similar course or workshop in your area.

Before committing to a course you need to make an informed choice and thereby you will limit disappointment. Ensure that you ask for a course programme, which should include information regarding the modules, the dates, how to pay, payment options and details of any concessions that may be available.

Some of the advantages of going on a course are:

- You receive a basic framework to function within which you can then restructure into your own way of working.

- You are taught the Code of Practice and how to implement it.

- You meet like-minded people.

- A support system should be available to you during and after you complete the course. This is because once on a course, unexpected emotions and irrational urges may come to the fore and need be dealt with. Providing support at such times should be part of the curriculum.

- You receive impartial feedback and input from fellow students.

- You become qualified.

Some of the basic challenges of going on a course along with the positive side are:

- It may be a substandard course. Under these circum-stances, Spirit is testing you with regard to assertion.

---

7 The College of Psychic Studies:
http://www.collegeofpsychicstudies.co.uk

- You may feel constrained by the ethos held by the principal, in which case the issue of discipline is being raised.

- The course fees may be expensive when travel, text- books, equipment and in some cases, accommodation is included. If necessary enquire about concessions.

- The course may exacerbate or sort out issues such as working under pressure, previously unidentified, a learning disability, or it may raise limitations due to a physical impairment. If there is a good support system then going through such challenges can enhance your work as a psychic.

- Being influenced by another student or facilitators' way of working. This may lead to self-doubting when developing personal methodology. It may also be the key to identifying your way.

- The course may fold halfway through, in which case it is showing it was not the course for you despite the fact you thought it was.

- The course may not meet your own expectations. This being the case, you need to reconsider why you feel as you do.

Before enrolling, it is wise to make detailed enquiries, ideally requesting an appointment with the principal and/or the facilitator. Even though you may have read the information in the course programme, ask again the following questions:

- What is the fundamental ideology of the centre/tutor are?

- How is the course run?

- What experience do the facilitator/tutors have?

- How long has the organisation been going?

- What psychic organisations are they affiliated to?

- Do they have insurance cover whilst you are a student?

- Is there an insurance arrangement you can take advantage of once you obtain your qualifications?

- Do they provide concessions to reduce the fees etc? Make sure you get any such agreement in writing before you pay.

- Is there an interest free monthly payment scheme?

- Do they give a refund if it is shown that the course is falling short in its programme?

When on a Course

The majority of students settle into a course without experiencing any problems at all. Some may feel that after having enrolled or after they have started the course it isn't for them. If you find you are one of these people it is best, before cancelling or leaving, that you first consider if the course itself is bringing up personal issues that you need to deal with. Most students' first emotional response to this process is to transfer their insecurity and confusion onto a tutor, another member of the class or blame the course itself. If you are not prepared to face such challenges, think very carefully about whether you should go on a course at all.

On the other hand, it could be it's a lousy course, only time will tell.

If the Course Doesn't Work for You

If you are sure it isn't your own issues being raised, you need to voice your concerns based on non-emotional facts to the principal as soon as possible. This will combat a principal's inclination to tell you it is your issues being raised that are causing the problems.

If your concerns are not taken on board and dealt with in a satisfactory manner, then obviously you need to request a refund, unless you unintentionally signed away your right to do so when signing up on the course.

The Pros and Cons of DIY

Not opting for professional training means working directly with Spirit without any buffers, which come in the form of facilitators and other students.

'Do It Yourself' is what it says – teaching yourself. There are just as many challenges and positives to DIY as going on a course. Some of the basic advantages to consider are:

- You can choose when it is convenient to you to develop your gifts.

- You are not influenced by other psychics' ways of working.

- There are no fees to pay.

- You can multi-task, which means developing more than one of your psychic abilities at a time.

- You do not have to adjust to someone else's framework before structuring your own way of working.

- You can form your own support system.

- You become qualified through experience, not a piece of paper.

144

Some of the disadvantages that may arise from not signing up for a course are:

- You do not receive a basic framework to function within, and from which you can restructure your own way of working.

- You cannot meet the challenge of working within the defined structure that a course provides.

- You are not taught the Code of Practice and how to implement it, but you can look one up on the internet.

- You may not get an opportunity to meet likeminded people 'on tap' so to speak.

- There may be difficulty in developing a reliable and effective support system.

- You are not being challenged by the accepted concepts and definitions of the course.

- You may not get impartial feedback and input from friends and family.

- You don't receive feedback from experienced psychics.

- You don't get a certificate.

If you decide not to go on a course, still consider making enquiries, for it is amazing how much you can learn from this simple exercise.

One of the major challenges for DIY'ers is to gain confidence in receiving and passing on messages in a cohesive, practical and logical manner. It is therefore imperative that a framework is developed to work within, in order to clear confusion that may arise.

A readymade framework would be tarot or runes since they use all the sensory and cognitive abilities we possess to contact, receive interpret and pass on spiritual messages.

Health, Anatomy and Physiology

In your role as a practising or professional psychic you will be asked to deal with health issues. Referring a client to a therapist or doctor is your first course of action. It is neither appropriate nor legal to diagnose, prescribe or comment about health issues unless you are qualified to do so.

Even so, a very basic knowledge of how and why the body works provides you with an additional skill that adds to your professional status. Doing an anatomy & physiology course will not go amiss. Obviously it helps if you are already a qualified therapist, counsellor or doctor, but the issue of not diagnosing or prescribing may still stand. Be prepared for people with life threatening conditions who seek hope from you. Please do not give false hope nor advise them of their demise, or when you sense it may be.

The Middle Way

There are times when you can have your cake and eat it too. Many people discover their psychic abilities whilst partaking in a complementary health course such as reiki, crystal therapy or colour therapy. Such courses are invaluable to the practising and professional psychic since they provide additional depth to any reading. Sue and Simon Lilly[8] run an array of such courses.

---

8 Sue and Simon Lilly: http://www.lilly-lilly.co.uk

24. Technique and Structure

Having a good reputation as a psychic reader depends upon technique and structure. Both enable a psychic to function as a professional. They are responsible for whether a new client will not only become a regular but also refer his or her friends to you.

Technique

Your reading technique has to be based upon your modus operandi, how you function naturally. Technique is built up of two components, accuracy and delivering the information clearly and precisely. Having confidence in your abilities to read, whether it be cards, people, energies or runes, ensures the information is accurate. The ability to deliver the information to your client in a clear, caring, logical, moral and ethical manner depends upon organisation.

Being a mixture of logic (which is left brain activity), and spiritual communication, (which is right brain activity) reading technique is developed by your:

• Personality.

• Knowledge of your craft.

• Life experiences.

• Ability to organise.

• Ability to learn from your clients.

Your reading technique is a part of who you are, but it is important to be flexible so you can adapt with each client's needs. The technique comes into play from when you answer the phone through to when you put it down. It involves:

- Your tone of voice – it should be caring but firm.

- The quality of your voice – clear pronunciation irrespective of your dialect. Your client needs to understand what you say.

- Your introduction - A client should be informed as to how you work in a clear and precise fashion.

- Your closing statements – advising your client that the reading is nearing the end and when it ends.

Horses for Courses

What is an acceptable technique for independent professional psychic readers may not be for a psychic agency. This is because the buck stops with the agency and therefore they have stringent guidelines to protect their business.

With an independent, the buck stops with the reader. Although strict sensible guidelines are essential, as an independent you will have far more leeway than when working for an agency.

Structure

Structure enables the reading to flow effortlessly from one topic (work, relationships, health and wealth) to another, without ostracising the client in the process. It is 'knowing' when to bring clarity into the reading and when to allow the messages from Spirit to come through unabridged. Structure is dealing with the unexpected in a balanced, organised and productive manner. It is formed by:

- Working through one topic at a time and then summarising.

- Avoid the temptation to jump from one topic to another and back again, unless there is a theme running through the reading itself.

- Interacting with the client during the reading by asking for feedback.

- Try not to ask too many questions, otherwise you are defeating the purpose of your craft. You are meant to be telling your client about their situation, not asking them.

- Maintaining control of the reading by keeping calm and focused when under duress.

- Dealing with the issues as the information received dictates rather than allowing the client to off load on you.

- Remembering you are a professional psychic, not their friend. As such you need to keep and maintain your distance.

- Avoiding mixing business with pleasure; otherwise be prepared for the consequences.

- Having the confidence to refuse to or stop a reading, in which case give a full refund.

- Refusing to predict even though you are asked to do so.

- Not allowing the client to place you in the position where they think you have it wrong, you haven't. You have hit a blindside, so rephrase or provide additional information.

- Not going on the defensive during a reading.
- Never reading when you are ill or over-stressed.

The Six Phases of Technique and Structure

By combining structure and technique you develop a minimum of six phases that can provide a professional quality to your readings.

The First Phase is a client's enquiry. It provides the client with the information he or she needs to know before deciding whether you are the right psychic for them. Be prepared to answer such questions as:

- How much do you charge?

- How long is the reading?

- What is your methodology of working? E.g. what divination tool do you use if any, and are you a psychic, medium, clairvoyant or all three?

- Dop you work with Tarot?

- How long have you been working as a psychic?

- Are you agency or independent?

The Second Phase is taking payment before the reading starts. The time to process the payment should not be included in the time allotted to the reading. Make a note of the time you start the reading.

The Third Phase is to write and deliver the introduction, which takes place before the reading starts. An introduction advises a client how you work and what they can expect from a reading. It needs to be informative, to the point and no more than five seconds. Although much of this is covered in phase one, not all clients start off with phase one and it is best to remind the client anyway. An example of an introduction is as follows:

- Your greeting (good morning, afternoon or evening)

- Your reading name.

- Your skill, whether you are a psychic and/or medium clairvoyant etc.

- How you work – e.g. "I work with … to receive and deliver the information you may need to be aware of. You are invited to interact but please allow the messages to come through first." Like taking payment, the introduction should not be included in the allotted reading time.

- Include a phrase that makes it clear you do not give comfort readings. Like taking payment, the introduction should not be included in the allotted reading time.

- Have an up-to-date list of head office telephone numbers of professional organisations that you can refer your client too. Tip: avoid recommending what you haven't tried first

The Fourth Phase is to start the reading and throughout recommend 'self-help' books or therapies that you feel would assist. Tip: avoid recommending what you haven't first tried yourself. Have an up-to-date list of the head office telephone numbers of professional organisations to hand so you can refer your client if necessary.

The Fifth Phase is the precursor to the closing statement and begins after you have finished the reading. This is when a client needs to be asked if he or she has any final questions. Allow approximately three minutes for this phase before the closing statement, which needs to only be a couple of seconds. A phrase such as, "We are coming to the end of the reading, do

151

you have any questions" will suffice.

The Six and Final Phase is the closing statement, the simpler the better: "That is the end of the reading, many thanks for your custom". A closing statement should not be included in the allotted reading time.

Bearing all the above in mind, a twenty-minute reading should last approximately twenty-three minutes and a thirty-minute reading should last about thirty-three minutes.

25. How to Divine

It has been my experience that anyone can read any divination tool if it is approached in the proper manner. Divination is a right brain activity because it works with limitlessness, intuition and "anything can happen" concepts.

I have chosen tarot as an interactive divination tool because it is one of the most comprehensive forms of divination and is readily available almost anywhere. It is also a wonderful partner when it comes to self-discovery, since it highlights the collection of selves within the Self.

The fundamental principles outlined in this chapter can be applied to any other form of divination. As for explaining tarot itself, I have given only the most basic information, which is based upon my interpretation, that which is right for me. It can be used as it is, or will complement any book dedicated to learning tarot.

Choosing a Pack of Tarot

Generally speaking, a pack of tarot is made up of 22 major arcana, 40 minor arcana and 16 court cards. The minor arcana and court cards are divided into four suits, cups (hearts), swords (spades) wands (clubs) and pentacles (diamonds). As you will see, the tarot suits correspond to an ordinary pack of playing cards.

There are hundreds of different tarot packs to choose from, so buying a pack of tarot can be quite bewildering. Therefore, allow your intuition to choose which is the one for you.

The different designs of tarot reflect different perspectives. Therefore the pictures depicted on the face of the cards will differ with each pack, but the four suits, symbology and fundamental meanings remain the same.

153

If you feel an immediate affinity or familiarity with the pack it means memories from when you were a tarot reader in a past life are resurfacing. This doesn't mean you can lay a spread for the first time and give an accurate, logical and informed reading. It means you may well pick it up quicker than someone without such an advantage.

If your confidence fails you, go with the Rider Waite, which is not only an excellent pack for learning but it evolves with you. A lot of professional psychics have started off and stayed with this pack.

Familiarising Yourself with the Pack

Getting used to handling and feeling the cards is important. During quiet moments, go through the pack three or four times shuffling them, then file them into their respective suits. The more you look at them the more you bond with the cards. Bonding with your cards is an integral part of learning tarot.

Then work through the pack and look at each of the pictures on the face of each card in detail; is the person looking at you or to the side? Are they carrying something, or not? such detail is relevant. Pick up each card, close your eyes and allow the card to speak to you or draw a vision in your mind.

You will find that tarot is nothing more than 78 picture cards that, when intermixed, can produce thousands of different images displayed in sequence to tell a story. The length of the story is dependent upon the number of tarot cards dealt in a spread.

A spread is in fact a storyboard which gives an allegorical representation of a situation at hand. It contains the nature of the challenges, the source of solutions and provides a vision of the 'Big Picture'.

The next step is, work with each card, writing down whatever comes into your head without referring to any text books.

154

After you have completed that exercise, compare what you have written with descriptions given in the remainder of the chapter. Do not concern yourself if you have a complete opposite, you are simply providing an alternative interpretation.

Keywords

Once you have familiarised yourself with your pack, compile your own list of keywords for each card of the pack. Include the keywords from numerology and astrology as well as tarot to provide depth and range.

Avoid comparing your keywords with anyone else's as it is like comparing chalk with cheese. Your version will be right for you but you may learn from another's keywords. My version of keywords can be found at the back of the book.

The Minor Arcana Suits

The minor arcana are associated with relatively minor issues and decision-making. Being multi-purpose the four suits represent:

- The four seasons - spring, summer, autumn and winter

- The four winds of direction - north, south, east and west

- The four elements - earth, air, fire, and water

- The four functions of the mind - thinking, feeling, sensation and intuition.

- The four worlds of creation - divine, creative, formative and manifest.

- The four humours - yellow and black bile, blood and phlegm.

NB. all of the above correspond to the four aspects of your life, which are relationships, health, work and wealth, which in turn correspond to four suits of the tarot. They are made up of:

- Pentacles (diamonds): summer, wealth, warmth, light, courage and sensation - represents the element of earth and represents materialism and financial issues, and some tarot readers include health in this suit. This suit is feminine in nature and is influenced by Capricorn, Virgo and Taurus.

- Wands (clubs): autumn, work, possibilities - represents the element of fire, which stands for work, career prospects, creativity, action, travel and movement. This suit is male in nature and corresponds with Aries, Leo and Sagittarius.

- Cups (hearts) : spring, life, happiness, joy, the centre of life and the world, relationships and value - represents the element of water and stands for matters of the heart, feelings, and some also include health, healing and psychic ability in this suit. It is female in nature and corresponds to Cancer, Scorpio and Pisces.

- Swords (spades) : winter, the cosmic tree, health and clarity - represents the element of air and stands for spiritual force communication; the mind, thought, deals with the abstract by providing definition and some consider this to also include psychic ability. They convey challenges and finding solutions through clarity by cutting through what causes confusion and blockages. With regard to health, it indicates acupuncture or a possible operation. This suit is male in nature and corresponds to Gemini, Libra and Aquarius.

There are four court and ten minor arcana cards to each suit. One of the easiest ways to get a basic understanding of the placement of the ten cards is to use numerology. Here is a technique that you may find helpful; using a plan to grow some flowers as an analogy.

Ace   The idea to plant some flowers (a vague idea).

2   Gathering the seeds and preparing the land (the idea is starting to take form).

3   Planting the seeds and watering them (the idea becomes a prototype design).

4   The shoots show above the soil (the prototype is developed).

5   The roots start to develop further (the working product is developed and the market is identified).

6   The plant takes form and buds appear (the product is being promoted).

7   The buds develop and bloom (the product starts to sell).

8   The flower is in full bloom (the product is selling worldwide).

9   The flower starts to wilt (the product becomes outdated).

10   The petals drop off exposing the seedpod, which is ready for gathering (the product is withdrawn from the market, but the next generation is prepared and ready to be launched).

The Court Cards

The court cards represent humanity and bring relevance and meaning to the reading by symbolising the four stages of the cycle of a life: childhood, adolescence, maturity and old age.

They represent sixteen personality types and correspond to friends, family, acquaintances, work colleagues and all those who cross your path throughout your life. As with people, court cards do not necessarily conform to the suit they represent at times.

Below is an elementary description of the meanings and definitions of the court cards and major arcana together with my placement of their respective personality types (PT)[9].

Characteristics of Pentacles: Black haired, brown-eyed person, a wealthy man, whether it is spiritually, emotionally, mentally or physically.

- King PT: ESFP. "The Performer". A man aged 40 or over, an executive or the head of a family. Is practical, uses logic and enjoys being the centre of attention. He can become overwhelmed at times and uses simplicity to deal with situations. Fun loving and he knows how to enjoy life. He is a "hands" on man and therefore may have tendencies towards being a control freak and stubborn. He may be over reliant on financial gain and is therefore insecure in who he is at times and gets lost in the financial bottom line rather than focusing upon how he got there. His intentions are good.

- Queen PT: ISFJ. "The Nurturer". A woman aged 40 and over, an executive or the head of a family. As is with the King, she is practical, uses logic, and is relatively stable, generous and kind. Has a tendency to be too kind - using generosity to keep the peace or gain and maintain control.

---

9   Myers-Briggs MBTI personality assessments and the earlier work of Jung. To discover more about your own personality: www.mypersonality.info has the Myers-Briggs test and many other tests.

- Prince PT: ISFP. "The Artist". A young boy/man aged between 0 and 39 may well come from a wealthy family, a classic tall dark, attractive personality, sensitive, creative, intelligent and full of potential, but is often troubled, frustrated, broody. A tendency to work on the shallow levels and behave like a spoilt brat when he feels he can't cope.

- Princess PT: INTP. "The Thinker". A young girl/woman aged between 0 and 39, may well come from a wealthy family. She has an attractive personality and an optimistic outlook, a free spirit, full of ideas and a constructive dreamer. Feels most comfortable theorizing, and may find it hard to put into practice her idea or find difficulty finishing what she has started. This lady is usually very tolerant, leans towards shyness, but needs her own space and will snap if pushed too far or feels crowded. She has firmly held beliefs and when challenged can become intolerant and rigid. She may also have a tendency to over achieve since she is not usually in tune with those around her.

Characteristics of Wands: Strawberry blonde/red-headed, green eyed people, who are creative and enjoy excitement, may well have a tendency towards being adrenaline junkies.

- King PT: ENTJ. "The Executive". A man aged 40 and over. Is able to climb the corporate ladder, if he hasn't done so already. A natural provider. May have tendencies to be a workaholic or hide behind work, using it as an excuse not to work in a relationship or take his rightful place within the family. Can have a bad temper, which he uses to gain control over others by being mentally, emotionally and verbally abusive if not physically threatening or violent if his anger isn't managed.

- Queen PT: INTJ. "The Scientist". A woman aged 40 and over. A very active woman, who questions. This lady enjoys using her mind and being kept occupied. Very good career prospects but may well suffer from being an over achiever when young and could have feelings of guilt if trying to balance career with motherhood. Such people can snap in frustration at times due to work-load and finds it hard to delegate.

- Prince PT: ESFJ. "The Caregiver". A young boy/man aged between 0 and 39. Full of potential, his mind works very quickly, to others it may appear that he finds it hard to focus least of all stay still for five minutes, but this may not be the case. He is very sensitive and caring. He is interested in people and can see what needs to be done, takes things seriously and is dependable. May suffer from a temper due to frustration and can turn at a moments notice from being a vibrant, fun loving young man to an angry person who could turn to becoming mentally, emotionally and verbally abusive, if not physically threatening or violent if his anger isn't managed.

- Princess PT: ENTP. "The Visionary". A young girl/woman between aged 0 and 39. Works well with thinking up new ideas, but may find it hard to implement them. May well suffer from being an over or under achiever. Has the ability to climb the corporate ladder but may suffer from a lack of confidence. May snap due to frustrations of not being taken seriously or understood and may have difficulty communicating in a clear logical manner at such times.

Characteristics of Cups: Light-haired, blue eyed people who are the romantics, the dreamers rather than the doers, never the less can be successful in any form of creative role.

- King: PT: ENFP. "The Inspirer". A man aged 40 and over. A person to whom relationships can be very important, has good people skills. He can work well in a partnership whether it be work or relationships but doesn't function best on his own. Needs to be true to himself and therefore has the ability to inspire others. A kind, caring and loving man who believes family is more important than climbing the corporate ladder. For all the best intentions in the world he may well be too laid back at times, have a tendency to be late or unreliable and emotionally unstable at times. May find it difficult to handle finances.

- Queen PT: INFJ. "The Protector". A woman aged 40 and over. This lady is intuitive, follows her instincts, can empathise with others, will be there to help in an instant due to her caring nature. This lady may find it difficult to take responsibility to assert, can internalise conflict and may not handle assertion and conflict well. A natural mum, who feels more comfortable in a homely environment rather than a career and runs the risk of having children to justify her existence rather than recognising there is life after motherhood. May have a tendency to 'mother' adults.

- Prince PT: INFP. "The Idealist". A young boy/man aged between 0 and 39.The Romeo, a kind person, intuitive, tends to look for the best of a situation rather than looking at a situation as a whole. He genuinely feels deep emotions but loves the process of falling in love but may not be that good at working in a relationship. If a relationship doesn't come up to his expectations - and no relationship can - he may blame his partner rather than look at his unrealistic expectations. Thinks well of himself and leans toward being a little narcissistic and lazy by naturally looking at the easy way of doing things or not doing anything at all it if looks like hard work, when feeling underconfident.

- Princess PT: ENFJ. "The Giver". Young girl/woman aged between 0 and 39. A very caring, focused person, who genuinely wishes to assist and may have a natural leaning towards a 'caring' profession. This person has a tendency to be manipulative, although there is no doubt she can see how things could be. This means she can be strong willed and controlling at times. It is important for this person to take time out to recoup. Their ability to manipulate may lean toward laziness if not checked.

Characteristics of Swords: Brown haired blue/brown eyes, people who are logical, academic, emotionally closed but are reliable, have good communication and the ability to override their emotions at times when emotions are not appropriate.

- King PT: ESTJ. "The Guardian". Man aged over 40. This person feels comfortable in a rational logical environment. He has a good wit, enjoys clever jokes that are often derived from factual incidents and his enjoyment of the language combines with quick instincts, which may at times be inappropriate. He would make a good surgeon or lawyer or hard-nosed businessman. However, his over reliance on fact means he can unwittingly hurt people at times and his need for security means he may be too rigid in his outlook or even become obsessive. He can also be verbally abusive and has the ability to cut a person into ribbons with only a couple of sentences. Tends to enjoy his own company and definitely needs his own space if in a relationship. Although distant, he sees his role as a provider and would do all he can to provide for his family. May well be a disciplinarian and find it hard to bond to his children or have an emotionally based relationship with his partner.

- Queen PT: ISTJ. "The Duty Fulfiller". A woman aged over 40. This lady can be loyal, dependable and law abiding. She is intelligent, has many interests but needs security and a peaceful environment within which to function at her best. However she may take many aback with her directness but most would find this directness a breath of fresh air. This lady will not let something go until it has been resolved. Although she is clever, focussed and knows how to put her case forward this lady can have an issue when saying "no" at times. Some men, who are not comfortable in themselves, may find her challenging and she may go on the defensive and become difficult to interact with at such times. Not very tolerant of those who do not pick up quickly or see the grey in a situation.

- Prince PT: ISTP. "The Mechanic". A young boy/man between 0 and 39. This person is a 'needs to know' person, as a consequence may have a tendency to take charge of things despite his years and inexperience. He is able to identify and solve problems both efficiently and quickly. Doesn't suffer fools gladly and tends to ignore those who know more than he. Such people can't take advice and need to find out for themselves. This person may well be a difficult person to interact with at times since he can interpret kindness as weakness, may not keep to the rules and can tend to be both judgemental and hypocritical when feeling out of his depth.

- Princess PT: ESTP. "The Doer". A young girl/woman between 0 and 39. This person works in the here and now but still has the ability to work in depth, sees what is hidden and what isn't apparent to those around her. This gift can be both a blessing and a curse. Can act as a catalyst for those who do not wish to face facts or who are in denial. Those who do not understand where she is coming from unfairly judge this lady. This lady's priority is to get the job done, and therefore she may not take time to consider the rules and regulations and just go ahead, either with disastrous consequences or a phenomenal outcome. She can be very direct at times and her enthusiasm and willingness to act, if not checked, can be misinterpreted and may cause problems at times. She may also have a tendency not to think before she speaks and when she speaks, her quick wittedness sometimes gets her into trouble despite the fact that what she has said is actually true. It is not what she says but how she says it that gets people's backs up. Although I have included the age and physical description of my interpretation of the court cards, please do not become enslaved by them or any one else's description. Bear in mind you can have an older man with a young heart and a young woman who possesses the knowledge of an old soul.

Information that comes through to you and does not correspond with or is contrary to the orthodox meaning of the card should never be dismissed. Instead, include it or allow it to take precedence, since this is your intuition at work.

Once you have a basic understanding of the minor arcana and the court cards, focus upon the major arcana, using the same process.

The Major Arcana

You will notice that the major arcana fall outside of the suits and are known as trumps, which is derived from the word, 'triumphs'. When applied to tarot they represent the triumphs of the human condition as well as its betrayal. They do so in the form of twenty-two archetypes, which represent 'the original' and is can be used to highlight and represent personality traits and mythical beings. The major arcana also represents the major decision-making involved in life changing events.

Again, the pictures are made up of symbolic elements that are the archetypes depicted on the card. Within that picture are representations of an ideal or ideals. The major arcana represent:

0. The Fool – Personality type ESFP. "The Performer." The Fool represents endings and new beginnings. With his or her worldly belongings held on the end of a staff, this mystic dreamer doesn't need a home in this world; since he or she can remember his or her home is in heaven. The dog, apart from being a valuable ally, keeps the Fool 'real'. It symbolizes knowledge, the natural world and the path represents the path to knowledge. This card is about self-responsibility and not allowing appearances to deceive.

The Fool walking off a cliff, which appears on the surface to be a foolhardy thing to do, represents an individual who looks as if he or she may not be looking where they are going. In fact it is quite the opposite. This person is taking a leap of faith, imbuing faith in him/herself and therefore in Spirit.

Only when a person has self-knowledge and a realistic understanding of personal limits do they have such faith in themselves. Having made the necessary appraisals before acting and prepared accordingly, this person knows that when they step off the cliff they cannot fall to their metaphorical death when they walk off the cliff's edge.

It also represents a person who is foolhardy, acts before thinking or assumes something is a lot easier than it actually is and as a result he or she doesn't prepare and is taken unaware. As a consequence they will simply fall to their metaphorical death.

1. The Magician (aka the Juggler and Magus) Personality type INTJ. "The Scientist." This person has a golden ball in his or her right hand, in the left a wand. In some cards, a hat in the shape of a sideways eight, the mathematical sign of infinity, is seen levitating above his or her head. The raised right hand represents activity, and the left pointing down to the ground shows passivity. Combined they show the sign of force, stability and the sense of self.

In front of the Magician is a table, which shows all the symbolic tools of the trade. These tools are the symbols of the minor arcana, the wand, pentacle, cup and sword, which are used to conjure up different opportunities and reveal secret realities. These symbols can also be shown being juggled effortlessly by the Magician as he or she carries out the work in hand.

The Magician uses creative energy and movement to carry out actions whilst maintaining focus and employing objectivity. The Magician doesn't self-doubt and has confidence in the ability to use personal power - because the Magician knows that his or her actions can determine the out -come. This card is associated with a person who is practical and has the ability to act with logic and precision, thus enabling the desired result.

Alternatively, this may be a person who is so arrogant and ignorant that they deceive themselves into thinking they can achieve an out come without taking the necessary steps.

2. The High Priestess (aka the Papess) – Personality type ENFP. "The Inspirer." Usually shown as a priestess sitting on a throne or standing and is often depicted as wearing a veil. Sometimes she is seen to wear a horned diadem, a crown or head-band worn by Eastern monarchs. There is a globe centered between the horns and she wears a breastplate. At hand is an open book, at her feet the moon, which is associated with the occult and wisdom. This lady is passive yet strong and assertive, the eternal woman. She is placed between two pillars, which represent the Temple of Solomon, with one black, the other marked 'J' and 'B' the initials of Joachin and Boaz. There are also pomegranates, which are associated with Solomon and the Temple of Solomon.

The High Priestess represents intuitiveness, knowingness, wisdom, common sense and other-worldliness and can intervene with the use of both her intuition and knowledge to make sound judgments.

Alternatively she can represent a person who, despite their highly developed intuition, is impatient, thinks she knows better and intervenes when it is not appropriate to do so.

3. The Empress – Personality type ISFJ. "The Nurturer." Sometimes shown with wings, other times as being pregnant,

the Empress is a lady who is depicted as sitting on a throne or standing and surrounded by grain, which represents her power over abundance and creativity. She wears a crown of 12 stars, which represent Mother Nature and her dominance over it. Holding a sceptre in one hand, she represents a sensual being who has the power to give life. Some cards show an eagle in the right hand and in the left, a scepter. The eagle is symbolic of both soul and life.

The Empress is associated with material prosperity, the finer things in life, including comfort and pleasure but not at the expense of nature and a healthy lifestyle. Creativity comes in many forms, not only the ability to create, carry and give birth to a child. The Empress is associated with great courage, sacrifice and all forms of creation as well as Mother Nature, Gaia herself. Therefore she is the epitome of all things patient and nurturing.

Although strength and forbearance is the mainstay of the Empress, with these self same qualities she can also be ruthless, dogmatic and dangerous - hell has no fury like a woman scorned.

4. The Emperor – Personality type ENTJ. "The Executive." Usually depicted as sitting on a throne, either sitting side profile or facing the reader. He is both unreachable and ruling from afar. Associated with King Minos, he wears either a crown or a helmet with twelve stones. In his right hand he holds a sceptre in the shape of an ankh, which represents life and shows that he is a figure of authority; as it is he that makes decisions of life and death.

Although often set rigid in his thinking, the Emperor represents the positive and challenging aspects of the male prerogative, ultimate ego, pride and dominance; yet he is still someone a person can aspire to become. He can also represent a situation or a challenge that has yet to be met. This is a card of needing to assert and gain control of one's life rather than being controlled and therefore needing to be in control of others.

The Emperor is also associated with reliability, stability and self-worth. This is a person who can be a force of nature for the better good of all or for very selfish reasons due to stubbornness, fear of failure or simply because he is unable to see the need for compromise.

5. The Hierophant (aka Pope) – Personality type ISTJ. "The Duty Fulfiller." The Hierophant is shown wearing a triple crown, which to some represents the three in one mystery when worn. An educated and knowledgeable person in his/her own right. The right hand is usually being raised and with two fingers pointing toward the sky is the sign used to give a blessing. Two fingers pointing down show that he/she is a bridge between the cosmos, which represents where Divine Spirit resides, and earth - the home of humanity.

Although representing the status quo, institutions and social convention, the Hierophant can also be shown leaning on a papal cross. He/she usually sits or stands between two columns; the right stands for law, the left for freedom and he/she represents the five senses. At his/her feet lie the keys of the Cosmos, which can be used to gain access to Divine Spirit.

Some depictions show two men kneeling before him, one is red, the other black.

The Hierophant is associated with spiritual knowledge. He/she has the ability to interact with Spirit and live a spiritual based life where one 'walks their talk'. It is also the card of hypocrisy since he represents religion and orthodox theology as well as a "person of high social standing". In other words, "Do as I say, not as I do".

6. The Lovers –ESFJ. "The Caregiver." This card shows a man, who also represents the female's male aspect, and a woman, also the male's female side. Both are seen in union or holding hands, standing on a corner where two streets merge into one. This card represents the relationship you have with yourself and then with others.

There is often a sun or the representation of the sun god,

which is associated with the intoxication of love and the affect it has on two people as well as personal beliefs and value systems. It is associated with temptation and material attraction based on beauty and sex as well as an affinity with and bonding to each other based upon mutual respect and understanding.

This card is associated with choice, the difficult decisions associated with it, tolerance, compromise and acceptance. It also infers doubts are being raised with regard to decisions already made. The Lovers highlights the fact that unless people learn to love and accept themselves they cannot love and accept another. It recognizes that unless both parties learn to compromise, the one that does, compromises his or herself by default. It is a card of boundaries and what happens when a person's boundaries are not in place.

7. **The Chariot** – Personality type ESTP. "The Doer." This card shows a conqueror, a person who is in control, effortlessly driving a chariot pulled by two horses or sphinxes, one of which is black, the other white and are associated with contradiction. The charioteer may have an eight star crown associated with Venus and a square on his/her chest which represents the four corners of the earth.

It takes a lot of skill to drive a chariot but, if you look closely at the charioteer, he or she makes it appear to be easy. Only with practice, dedication and self-control can someone become that skilled.

Therefore this card is associated with self-responsibility and self control it reminds us nothing is as easy as it looks - gaining control is one thing, but maintaining it is another. To tke care not to become arrogant and egotistical due to past successes, otherwise control will be lost and the consequences will have to be met.

This card is also associated with honour, courage, being focused and in control. The charioteer represents an internal or external battle that can be or has just been won. Having identified their goal, this person has devised a realistic plan of action, which he or she has carried out. It is also a card of traveling and independence, and is associated with leaving home and being prepared to meet the trials and tribulations of life. This is one of the reasons why the card is often depicted with a bow and quiver of arrows close to the person's chest.

The Chariot is a person who oozes confidence but may also be impulsive at times despite his ability to focus. When focus is lost, this person becomes dangerous, an accident waiting to happen. Anyone who is in his or her path will be run over, by default.

8. Justice – Personality type INFJ. "The Protector." The concept of Justice is represented by a woman standing or sometimes sitting, and wearing a coronet. Often blindfold, she holds a sword in her right hand and a pair of scales in her left. The sword represents a willingness to fight for justice, and the scales represent meting out justice in a balanced, impartial manner. Justice is associated with the goddess Athena and as such she is also associated with not allowing the carrying out of justice to lead toward vengeance. In the case of justice, it takes a person who can remove their emotional bias, feelings and opinions from the situation and instead use reason, logic and objectivity to ensure that justice prevails. This card is associated with an injustice needing to be righted; court cases, compromise and being able to take responsibility for one's own actions. It also highlights the importance of balance and the role it has to play in any decision making and resulting actions.

9. The Hermit – Personality type INTP. "The Thinker." This card depicts a solitary, cloaked and sometimes hooded old man or woman with a staff in hand and with his or her back turned, walking away. The staff also represents a mobile altar, so some consider the Hermit to also be a traveling holy man who carries sacred items with him. This method was used in spreading the word in both pagan and early Christian times until churches with fixed altars become established.

This person carries a lighted lamp, which represents a wisdom that can only come from being prepared to face and deal with his or her issues. This person has a philosophical attitude and shows that he or she can tolerate their own company. They will accommodate others but feel they do not need them as they walk their path. This person has learned, and has started to put those learning curves into practice. Although still in the process of learning, this person can act as a positive example for all those who wish to follow.

The person has learned by working with silence, introspection and reflection that he or she can search within and find the answers. As the Hermit walks he or she gives a warning that retreat and renewal are necessary for growth but too much isolation, or withdrawing for the wrong reasons, can only stop personal growth.

10. Wheel of Fortune – Personality type ISFP. "The Artist." This card is also associated with the astrological cycles and karmic wheels of life. The wheel is a circle, no one knows where it begins or the ends, and it therefore symbolizes a never-ending process. Some decks show lettering or the alchemical symbols of earth, fire, air and water on the spokes of the wheel.

Wheels are for turning and our actions do just that. As the wheel of fortune turns so do our individual fortunes, which increase and decrease with each half turn. It is associated with turning points and the unrelenting passage of time and life cycles.

The Wheel of Fortune provides hope of good fortune, a sign that it is time for new developments, activity and moving forward. It also dashes hope and brings us to the realization that false hope is another form of self-deceit. Nothing is given freely, only through hard work and dedication can we push the wheel forward. If we push too hard it will be self-defeating.

From the karmic perspective it is associated with what goes around comes around. The karmic wheel acts as a reminder that we never get away with anything, even if we think we have, that our actions can come back to haunt us. We rarely get what we want – but are provided with what we need, whether we want it or not. This card raises the issue of fate and destiny and our ability of being able to create our own destiny but only when we have identified our true desires and a reality that encompasses those desires.

11. **Strength (aka Fortitude)** – Personality type ESTJ. "The Guardian." It is represented by a young girl in control of a lion. This control is shown either by the girl riding the lion, as she would a horse, opening the lion's mouth or having the docile lion behind her.

This card has little to do with physical strength but rather strength of character. It shows that strength can be developed through moderation in all things when dealing with desire of any type. Neither wanting too much or too little, too soon or too late, nor avoiding whilst not actively wanting.

It takes great strength of character to be compassionate, show self-control and to be kind when having to assert. Strength is knowing when to walk the middle line of moderation. It comes naturally with age for some and is learned in the years of youth.

Strength is associated with both the discipline to do and not to do something. That serenity is the prize of moderation. Endurance is also strength, along with tolerance and the ability to identify and focus upon other peoples strengths rather than their weaknesses.

Without developing strength of character a person is vulnerable and they can fall into the pit of despair.

12. **The Hanged Man.** Personality type INFP. "The Idealist." (This card should not be confused with the practice of hanging a person upside down by one foot from a tree for horse stealing). Some associate this card with Norse mythology, specifically Odin, the god of those hanged for sacrificial purposes, who is associated with magic, poetry and wisdom. A person is shown hanging upside down from a tree by one leg, the other crossed to make an up-side-down figure four, which is associated with foundations. The person's hands are tied but there is no look of distress, which infers they have willingly placed themselves in this position.

It is associated with being able to look at things from a different perspective, even if it means a 180 degree turn around. Such a turnaround usually takes sacrifice in one form or another but the reward is to be able to look at life from a different perspective.

This means a person is willing to surrender, letting go of the 'Little Picture', in order to see how it really is in the 'Big Picture'. This card also represents a person who is open to change and willing to be suspended in mid air in order to receive new insight. This is a process that in itself is not easy but can enable a person to achieve what appears to be at first impossible. But only if he or she has the foresight and courage go through such a challenge.

The Hanged Man can also represent a person who has given up, is not prepared to put in the effort, and may not even be aware that they are looking at things 'topsy-turvy'. It is also a reminder that you can't continually choose to go against the tide without causing harm to yourself. Instead ,you lose the advantages originally gained by such action.

13. Death – Personality type ENTJ. "The Executive." This is a card of spiritual renewal. Tied into Saturn's return it is associated with the ending of one cycle and the beginning of another: A clearing of the tables to start again. It is not associated with physical death which is represented by a card in the minor arcana.

A skeleton is often depicted in this card dressed as a reaper, or as a king in black armour carrying the black banner of the Mystic Rose. The Mystic Rose is a symbol of secret doctrines that herald psychological transformation.

Whether it is the skeleton king or reaper, this card is associated with ego and the self; the need to keep one's ego in check whilst accepting the need to consciously work with change. This is the card of realization, to realize that no one can stop or avoid change. If he or she attempts to do so they will achieve nothing and will create problems for themselves that didn't previously exist.

This card highlights that change is not easy for anyone. That avoidance of change is an instinctual reaction, but unless it is overcome it places us in a fear-based life. It is a learning curve we all go through more than once in our lives.

The Death card is reminding us that wherever there are endings there are always new beginnings.

14. Temperance – Personality type ISTP. "The Mechanic." This card depicts a young person of androgynous nature standing by a stream or lake, (being outside rather than in a room symbolizes the element of air). This person is pouring water or some form of liquid from one chalice or jug to another. One foot is on the land (the element of earth) the other in the water (the element of water). Another picture shows this person having wings. The sun (the element of fire), is shining behind or above this person and in some cases it can give the impression of a halo appearing around the head. Temperance represents the bringing together of two opposites to create harmony and balance for all concerned. During this process a new element is being formed, this card is the principle of alchemy in motion.

On the surface of it, this action looks pointless. However, by looking closer you will find that something is being diluted, probably wine with water which symbolizes moderation and self-restraint. It shows that without self-discipline, a person cannot achieve their potential. It is also associated with the dangers of excess, whether it is a substance, thought or action.

Water is also associated with emotions and infers it is time to bring balance and harmony into one's life.

15. The Devil – Personality type ESFP. "The Performer." This card has nothing to do with the religious concept of the Devil. It highlights the ever-challenging side, the id, which lies within each one of us. The never-ending battle we all face not to fall into temptation.

This card also represents an inexhaustible source of energy, which comes from both the cosmos and the earth. For the purpose of tarot, it is depicted by a demon because no one is perfect. It is the second of the three cards that are associated with Saturn's return, the clearing of the tables to start again.

The right hand of the demon is shown raised to the heavens, the left pointing to the earth. There is a woman to the right and a man to the left of the demon and these people represent humanity. The pentagram is a pagan sign that represents the never-ending source of life force energy that is available to us all. It is such a powerful symbol because it's function is to draw in and distribute universal energies. It is not the sign of the devil. It has nothing to do with devil worship, death or inferring that a person is going to the orthodox religions concept of "hell."

When the point of the pentagram is facing down, it represents the cosmic energy which is continually being drawn from the cosmos to be grounded by the earth. When the point of the pentagram is facing upward, it represents the Earth's energy being directed into the cosmos. The pentagram shows that the earth and the cosmos are interdependent.

Although now demonized in many quarters, the horned goat headed, part human, part animal known as Baphomet is a sigil. It represents the universal union between positive and challenging energies. It is comparable to the yin and yang symbol of Tao.

The word Baphomet is thought to mean the absorption of knowledge. Often shown wearing a pentagram pointing down as a crown, Baphomet in tarot is associated with disassociating yourself from unhealthy lifestyles, peoples and habits.

It shows that a person can create a living hell on earth for him- or herself when they do not take responsibility for their own actions. By doing so, they can emerge from their self-produced hell.

16. The Tower (aka Fire) – Personality type ENFJ. "The Giver." This is the third and last card that is associated with Saturn's return, the burning tower. It presents sudden change and resulting chaos, which can be interpreted as a person's downfall or life-changing experience, depending upon how they respond to change.

This card shows a tower being struck by lightning and on fire. There are either people jumping from the windows or running away from the fire, which can represent a person's private hell and not hell itself.

The Tower represents a lifestyle or situation, neither of which is void of danger. It is the ability to recognize when a situation is no longer viable and make the necessary changes. Alternatively, it may show a refusal to believe change is coming and suffer accordingly. The Tower highlights that nothing stays the same. That there are two types of change; that which is the result of world events and that which is the result of a person's decision making and resulting actions.

The Tower is also associated with the concept, 'the higher you climb the harder you fall.' The coming down is inevitable and you can either come down on your own volition or wait until someone pushes you off your perch.

17. The Star – Personality type ISFP. "The Artist (II)." This is a card of renewal and is depicted by a naked woman who is pouring water from two jugs. The water is associated with emotions and love and the action itself shows love is in abundance and is 'free flowing' in nature. Water is being poured into a pond, which represents our subconscious, so this is also to do with the necessity to love ourselves at a subliminal level if we wish to meet and exceed our potential as human beings. The woman has one foot in the water, the other on land - the conscious material self. It is a card of renewal, hope and faith in one's abilities. There are seven stars, associated with the Seven Sisters (Pleiades), clustered around a larger star, which represents the self.

This card also holds with the saying, "you're a star". Itreminds us that we are made from star-dust, that the Higher-self still resides in the cosmos and is there to assist the Self along its journey. It also shows that it's time to raise our own expectations about ourselves and look to what we can achieve with realistic optimism.

Alternatively, we view the stars as being unreachable; we do not look up and cannot or do not try to raise our expectations. We accept 'what we are given' and by doing so we cannot identify or fulfil our true purpose.

18. The Moon – Personality type ENFP. "The Inspirer (II)." The moon represents nocturnal activity. It shows a path with a pillar on either side and a moon with a face on it; all of which represent the gateway to what is hidden, metaphysics, the psychic realms, the unknown and the subconscious, these all belong in the domain of the dark side of the moon. The movement of the moon is complex and some cards show the sixteen waxing rays. It highlights the importance of the effects waxing and waning have on nature, including human behavior, which is not recognized by many, but those who do understand are often associated with witches and vampires. There is a dog and a wolf, both of which represent our innermost fears. Some dogs bark at the moon because they can see it but cannot smell it and therefore cannot recognize what it is. A crayfish crawls out of the water onto the land. This is a reminder of our human origins and that we all come from the sea; being water, it too represents emotions.

The moon highlights a person's ability to deceive themselves and therefore deceive others. It is associated with the subconscious and the pre-subconscious, all of which are hidden, as well as the concept of shape shifting. With the moon comes doubt and confusion, clarity and certainty. What a person thinks in the day often takes on a different light at night.

It sparks the imagination and a remembrance of a time of running free and of releasing inner-most feelings. The moon is also associated with unrealistic ideas and fantasies which if not looked at in the clear light of day may well cause anxiety and self-deception.

19. The Sun – Personality type ENTP. "The Visionary." Showing two naked children, one a boy, the other a girl or two girls, either in the sun itself or the sun shining on them. This card represents optimism. It gives the message that with every sunrise there is a new day, renewal and with it new hope and opportunities. This card is also associated with spiritual rebirthing and physically giving birth.

The sun rules both consciousness and enlightenment and

therefore is also associated with mental, emotional, physical and spiritual success and well-being. It represents pure pulsating energy, transformation, personal power and the path that leads to true happiness, that of inner happiness. It is also associated with being too optimistic, arrogance, becoming delusional and egotistical.

20. **Judgment** – Personality type INFJ. "The Protector (II)." Is associated with how a person will be 'judged' and the answer is by his or her own actions. A karmic card, usually depicting a woman holding the scales of justice, it shows that justice is blind to the emotions and only focuses on a person's actions and the result of those actions.

Judgment is therefore made on the result of those actions and whether those actions have helped or destroyed. This card is associated with stopping, recognizing and accepting that we could have made better choices in the past. Reconciliation with self and others must happen so that renewal and redemption can take place, thus enabling a rebirthing and personal liberation to take place. It represents reserving judgment until all the facts are known. Judgment and Justice are not both sides of the same coin, they are two different coins.

It is also associated with judgmental people, an inability to compromise and the reluctance or refusal to accept responsibility. It can also be associated with lawyers, court cases and awaiting judgement.

21. **The World** – Personality type ENFJ. "The Giver (II)." The last card of the major arcana and as such one of fulfilment, of what is possible. This is shown by a naked woman or hermaphrodite with the head of a human, lion, ox, and eagle, all suspended above the earth and therefore 'in' the world but not 'of' the world. If shown, the four faces represent the faces of Matthew, Mark, Luke and John in the New Testament, and the four former and latter prophets in the Old Testament, and also the fixed signs of the zodiac: Aquarius, Taurus, Leo and Scorpio. Some decks may show this individual dancing and holding two staves, one in each hand, and when crossed they represent the four corners of the earth.

This card is also a representation of the earth, Gaia, who is surrounded by a green wreath or a snake holding its own tail, the sign of everlasting knowledge. Below are the earthbound creatures, including humanity, who watch her, the source of all creation. This card is associated with a person having the world at their feet, a privileged and hard fought for position that has been finally granted.

The above descriptions of the major arcana are, again, to be used as guidelines only.

The Tarot Spreads

As mentioned earlier, the spread is how the tarot cards are laid out and it is an allegorical representation of a situation in hand. The spread can accommodate a general or specific reading.

The spread is where the reader gains information about the querent, the name given to clients who wish to have their tarot read. Irrespective of the number of cards, it represents the querent's life in a story-board format.

A spread can confirm events and provide a choice of possible outcomes and where he or she stands within it at that present moment in time. It is multi-dimensional since it provides a beginning, middle and end, which correspond to the past, present and a potential, optional future. Don't forget the parallel universes as well.

There are many different spreads, which use varying numbers of cards, ranging from using one card to using the whole pack. What takes preference is the reader's choice of spread, the one he or she feels most comfortable with.

There are spreads that apply for every occasion or situation. There are vertical, horizontal, circular spreads and combinations of two or three simultaneously. For vertical spreads, bottom equates to the past, middle equates to the present and top equates to the future. For horizontal spreads, left equates to the past, midway to the present and right to the potential / optional future. Circular spreads represent the cycle of life – no one knowing where the beginning or end is. You will find your preference by experimentation and you can adapt the layout of any spread to suit your self.

If the reading is taking place over the phone, the reader selects the cards for the spread. If person-to-person, then it is the querent who should shuffle and select the cards and pass them to the reader to lay out in the spread.

For this purpose, the favoured spread is the Celtic Cross. It uses 10 cards, each numbered box represents a card and the layout is as follows:

Table XI The Celtic Cross					
	Past	Present	Future		
Future		3		Q. Full potential	10
Present	6	1 2 over	4	Who Q. may become Who Q. is now	9 8
Past		5		Who Q. was	7

Q. = Querent

The numbers represent the order in which the card is dealt and its placement.

Making Sense of a Spread

One of the best ways of learning to read from a spread is practical experience. Each card in the spread provides a visual layout of a non-specific event, which is to be interpreted by you, the reader. By connecting the interpretations of each card together a story and timeline is created, no matter how simple.

The process is very easy and only becomes complicated by getting bogged down by working with too much detail too quickly, or missing the obvious because it is so simple. Once a basic foundation is laid, the reader can build upon it by asking Spirit for further information and referring to the keywords to provide assistance with interpreting the symbology on the card.

Deal the spread of your choice. What you have in front of you is a representation of a complete multi-dimensional story, which can represent a reality. Take a few seconds to look at the overall spread and make a note of your own feelings and how they have responded to the spread itself. The pointers are:

- If, overall, the cards have a more red/orange quality than blue/green, it infers action.

- If blue/green is dominant it means inactivity and the spread is telling you that it's time to stop and reassess before acting.

- If there is a general mix it infers balance.

Bear this in mind whilst looking at the spread in detail then decide where to start; work, relationships, health or wealth.

Always be mindful that there is a very fine line between predicting, which is now illegal and relaying information received from spirit.

If reading for someone else, you may well go blank at

times, that really isn't a problem so long as you do not stop talking, instead have stock phases such as, "right, what am I seeing/ sensing/ hearing here", or, "I am going to go silent for a few seconds so I can work more in-depth on this one". Either the message will come or you can refer to your keywords to give you a kick-start.

If a suit is missing, it is just as important as if there was a dominant suit showing. A suit that isn't there can mean hard work and hidden opportunities, while a dominant suit can mean there may be opportunities that are too good to be true – or that it is time to act.

Focus on the major arcana; more than one major arcana can infer a time of major decision-making. If none are dealt, it's a time of minor decision-making. Experiment with different types of spreads during this phase to familiarise yourself with the process of reading from a spread. This includes doing daily and individual spreads.

Always look out for contradictions with what you said earlier since it shows that the issue needs to be looked at again. Contradiction in messages shows that you are revealing confusion, whether it is with the querent, the reader or both, or that the situation itself is confusing. It can also indicate that there is a choice. Don't concern yourself, contradiction can and does happen to the most experienced of professional psychics and is a valid way of working as long as you know how to work through it.

Experiment with different types of spreads during this phase to familiarise yourself with the process of reading from a spread. This includes doing daily and individual spreads.

Daily Spreads vs. Individual Spreads

Professional telephone readers can deal one spread for the day or do a different spread for each individual.

The daily spread attracts and highlights the individual needs of those who phone that day. The same card will bring forth a different message for each querent. You will not be repeating the same messages because each querent is different. This process is another excellent example of the hyper-communications network in motion.

Individual spreads are when you deal a spread for each querent. They are no better than the daily spread and the same cards may be dealt no matter how well you shuffle. It is simply an issue of preference of the reader.

Practice, Practice, Practice

Before you let yourself loose on the general public, make sure you get plenty of reading practice. There are two ways of practicing with a querent - using a dummy or a friend. Below is the procedure for both.

The same care and attention needs to be applied to practice readings as when you are reading as a professional psychic. This means setting yourself up by getting a table large enough to deal a spread, an egg timer, pen, paper and a tape recorder. Record the readings, even when you are using a dummy querent. Recording the readings from day one of practice provides you with a record of your progress and helps with developing your technique and structure..

A Procedure to Practice Tarot Readings Using a Dummy for a Querent

First, find a cushion, doll or teddy bear or a picture of a model from a magazine to represent your querent. Your intention will bring in a spirit guide to interact with you. It will make itself known to you through visions or words in your head, but scepticism will block the entity from participating. Then set yourself up and programme the egg timer for five minutes. Below is a procedure that does work for those who know that it can:

- Place your dummy querent in a chair opposite you and position it where you would ask a live querent to sit to have a reading with you.

- Have your opening and statement and to hand if you haven't memorised it, along with your cards and.

- Decide which spread you wish to use and shuffle the cards.

- Clear your mind.

- Deal the spread; I suggest you start with four cards.

- Look at the overall spread and make a mental note of the number of cards in the same suits and if all four suits are represented. If a suit is missing it is just as important as if there is a dominant suit showing. A suit that isn't there can mean hard work and hidden opportunities and a dominant suit can mean there may be opportunities that are too good to be true or that it is time to act.

- Look to see if many major arcana have been dealt and if so how many. More than one major arcana can infer a time of major decision-making. If none are dealt, it's a time of minor decision-making.

- Ask your dummy querent which topic they wish you to start working with; work, relationships, health or wealth. Whichever topic comes into your head first will be correct.

- Relax and focus on the cards whilst working with the topic.

- Look at the card that represents the past and focus on the picture and write down what is coming.

- If 'nothing' comes to mind, write down 'nothing'.

- Look the card up on the list of keywords and note them down.

- If you have a tarot book, read up the description of the card in the book, add a précised version to your own notes.

- Make a sentence from what is on your piece of paper.

- Go through this process with every card until you have completed the spread and covered all four topics.

- Read through all that you have written and string the information into an understandable sentence, statement or phrase for each topic.

TURN ON THE TAPE RECORDER

- Read out the information from your prepared reading. During this time you may receive additional information. Allow it to come through, but remember your timing for the session.

Then listen to the tape recording and make notes where you think you can improve your technique. Continue this procedure increasing the number of cards with each reading until you are able to read a full spread, which needs to be used for a 30-minute reading. Practice until pleased with the recording of a reading

A Procedure to Practice Tarot Readings with Friends or Family

It is important to respect the wishes of those who do not wish you to do a reading for them. Do not take it personally, since this is a very good learning curve for you to go through.

When you have found those who want you to do a reading for them make sure you get their permission to record the readings. Make it clear you will be keeping a copy but obviously offer to provide them with a copy. Then listen to the recordings when on your own.

- Set yourself up as you would with a dummy querent.
- Introduce yourself, even though you know the querent
- Make sure your querent is sitting comfortably and ask him or her to shuffle the cards several times.
- Ask the querent to choose and take out the number of cards required for the spread.
- Clear your mind.
- Deal the spread.
- Give yourself time to receive what is coming through intuitively from the spread, this should take no more than between 5 - 10 seconds but may take longer to begin with.
- Ask the querent which topic they wish you to work with first, work, relationships, health or wealth. If the querent asks for you to choose, it is up to you whether you do, but it's best to politely insist that they choose. Otherwise, it can leave you wide open to being told you haven't dealt the 'right' spread if the querent doesn't like the reading.
- Look at the overall spread, making a mental note of the number of cards in the same suits and if all four suits or any major arcana are represented.
- Start to describe what you are seeing, feeling sensing and/or hearing overall. Then ask the querent which of the remaining topics they wish you to focus on next. Repeat the process until you have covered all four aspects.
- Start to bring in the information but always include relevant common sense and logic to the message being received since they act as a caveat and prevent you from predicting. E.g. Querent: "Am I going to meet someone?" The spread shows a person is on the way in, so the answer is "Yes". Using common sense and logic, the answer is expanded to "Yes, but only if the querent develops a healthy social circle built on positive activities and hobbies can they create an opportunity to meet the person who is

shown in the spread".
- After each topic, ask the Querent if they have any questions. If "yes", work more with the card again to gain clarification. If nothing more comes through, say so but advise him or her it may well come through later on in the reading.
- When at the precursor to the closing statement, ask if there are any more questions. This is where there is a danger of you allowing the reading to over-run, so bear in mind the time limit. It is not wise to exceed the agreed time of the reading, otherwise it will be expected in future readings.
- Use your closing statement.

Going Public

Irrespective of which method you use to practice there will come a time when you become a licentiate reader: you can read tarot but you are not yet up to the standard of a professional reader. To become one you will need to practice reading for the general public rather than friends or family. One of the best ways to gain this type of experience is to offer a free reading or a reading for a nominal fee of £5.00. This is done by putting a card up in a mind, body and spirit shop or other suitable venues or maybe even arranging with the proprietors to do free readings.

Giving free readings provides you with a certain amount of leeway, but not as much as with family and friends. The general public are not stupid and reading for strangers is very different to reading for friends, family or a dummy. So how you conduct yourself whilst giving readings to strangers is very important.

Involve the querent at such times and be open and honest. They will appreciate it. If you don't understand a message say, "I don't understand what I am being given here, does it make sense to you?" If the message still doesn't make sense, ask them to put the message on the back burner and move on with the reading. You may well get additional information further on in the reading that pulls the message together. This usually happens, but it will be up to you to remind the querent and tie it into the reading. If not, you may well have hit a querent's blindside, in which case tact is needed.

Given time and experience reading for the general public you will find yourself developing your own meanings to the tarot and your own philosophy with regard to your spiritual growth. Both your meaning and your philosophy will be right for you. You will find that the way in which you work will attract the querents that can relate to your way of working. But others will not and that is their right.

At some stage you will need to start charging for the readings. Your fees should reflect your experience, but within reason. Before you know it you will be conducting yourself as a professional reader because you are one. By then you will be able to take onboard the complexities that are raised in readings, the majority of which relate to blindsides.

Back to Blindsides
At this stage you also need to bear in mind that some readings may reflect your own blindsides as well as that of the querent. Do not allow such issues to affect the reading and deal with what has been raised on your own, after the reading when you have time to reflect.

Blindsides are thought provoking and can be very confusing, difficult to accept and deal with for both the querent and reader. They are raised because the spread is multi-dimensional and therefore represents the past, present, future and parallel lifetimes, as well as past and future lifetimes.

A reader can unwittingly cross the threshold into a parallel or past life existence without realising it. Never the less, the information that comes through will always be correct.

If a querent cannot relate to a message they will think you have it wrong when in fact you have raised a blindside.

Assure them that you have questioned the validity of the message and have received confirmation that it should be delivered.

Let the querent know that the only valid and accurate explanation that can be given is that sometimes it can take years for the message to make sense – but, at other times, it can be revealed during the reading or shortly after it.

If the querent still needs an explanation it must be given by you, so don't lose your nerve because the querent has used their right to challenge the information you have provided them with. In order to handle this delicate situation, always bear in mind that we are all the sum total of our past as well as our past as well as our present lives, and therefore a message may come through that relates to a past life issue that he or she is still dealing with in this life time. The querent is now in a position to balance karma and/or go through a learning curve.

Put simply, the balancing karma is whatever happens to us, and that is a result of us doing to another what he or she is now doing to us in this lifetime. As a consequence, the whole process has created a blindside in this lifetime.

Under these circumstances, calmly but confidently explain to the querent – who may not like to think that they behaved in such a manner in a past life – that from the concept of reincarnation they did; otherwise they would not be enduring what they are.

Reassure the querent that there are no failures, nor mistakes. Remind them that all we do is to balance karma and go through learning curves. Point out that that the querent has a choice as to whether they wish to look further into the issue or not. Finally, suggest the querent put the issue on the back burner and that you move on with the rest of reading since further information may come through that will clarify the situation.

If the querent isn't able to do this and is insistent that he or she doesn't have such a blindside, it indicates that they may be going into denial. This in itself may prove that a blindside exists. At this point, do not allow the reading to degrade. Take the lead and suggest that you think it is wise to stop the reading, then discuss giving a partial or full refund.

Alternatively, you may be raising a blindside that the querent has already dealt with and it is no longer relevant. That being the case, they will let you know.

If the client is able to work with the concept presented to them, it is wise to bring in damage limitation by adding on, free of charge, the time spent dealing with the issue to the overall time of the reading. If you decide to give extra time then you need to advise the querent of this otherwise he or she may thing you have overrun by mistake.

As a reader, such readings are challenging but the experiences are invaluable. Nevertheless, you do need to consider how a querent will feel after they have put the phone down. There are usually four immediate reactions which are "That was a waste of time, what a con", "That was good, I will use that psychic again" or "I have certainly been given something to thing about, it has been challenging but refreshingly help helpful." The fourth is that a client may start to cry during or after the reading, but this will be a release.

26. Turning Professional

Trading Standards now refer to professional psychics as a Spiritual Service Providers. Turning professional means following an occupation that provides a livelihood for gain. Being professional is retaining one's objectivity and independence when dealing with a client.

It is up to the individual concerned to maintain the high standards that are expected from anyone who calls themselves a professional, irrespective of the field they work within. Otherwise, problems can occur. Problems cause disagreements, which can develop into disputes. Serious disputes can end up in court and can bring the profession into ill repute.

The organisation that can shoulder the responsibility of being a spiritual service provider is the Spiritual Workers Association (SWA) (http://www.theswa.org.uk). They can give you advice and support as and when necessary.

When problems do occur, and any realistic businessperson knows that they will, they need to be recognised and dealt with quickly rather than hoping 'the problem will go away'. 'Dealt with' means making a note of the name of the querent, the time and date of the reading and the nature of the dispute and then waiting for developments or giving a refund at the time the dispute occurs.

The Importance of Interpretation

Few professions enjoy as much freedom of interpretation as the professional psychic. With this freedom comes great responsibility.

All messages from Spirit are open to interpretation and all will be correct if they are given the time to unfold. This

191

principle applies even if one reading appears to contradict another since both represent a viable alternative reality. Knowing how to employ this fundamental difference shows whether you are working as a professional psychic or an amateur. Professionals do not predict, nor do they deliver the message without providing the client with a choice and placing them squarely in the frame as being the one who is responsible for making those choices.

Exchange of Energy

An "exchange of energy" is a quaint term used by some within the psychic profession to deal with the issue of receiving money for services rendered. This exchange occurs ahe minute a professional psychic receives financial payment for his or her services. This is also the time when d their spiritual wealth has been transformed into financial wealth. It is as simple as that. The next step is to maintain a balance between reaping what you can whilst maintaining your morals and ethics.

From the spiritual perspective, the exchange of energy is that which happens between the client and psychic. Every word being spoken during the reading results in an inevitable 'cause and effect' and an 'action or reaction' to those words. The intentions and meanings of words being exchanged are woven within the etherics by the respective Higher-selves of the client and reader. This weaving helps define the independent but inter-connected roles both parties play within the Divine Plan. As this weaving takes place the 'butterfly effect' comes into play on a conscious level.

The Butterfly Effect

The 'butterfly effect' is really too big for us earthlings to fully comprehend. We do have some understanding of it and can therefore appreciate the brilliance of the concept. The butterfly effect highlights the importance of our simplest thoughts and actions and the effects they have upon the workings of the earth.

For those who haven't already heard of this effect, it refers to the concept that one flap of a butterfly's wings can create tiny changes in the etherics which are played out in the earth's atmosphere. These changes may ultimately cause reactionary events such as changes in weather patterns, varying in intensity.

In other words, any minute movement of energy can cause a chain reaction which eventually results in a major event. This concept falls outside of Newton's third law of motion but not the Cosmic Laws of metaphysics.

Being a part of the hyper-communications network, the 'butterfly effect' concept shows that our thoughts and actions have purpose, are of consequence outside of our habitat and that we are all interconnected. Most of us are blissfully unaware of the consequences of our thoughts, words or actions outside of our immediate surroundings until we have taken responsibility for our existence. Even then our understanding is exceedingly limited.

When doing a reading, it may be wise to bear this concept in mind without becoming paranoid. This is because psychic readings change lives for the better or worse and they do so partly because of the 'butterfly effect'. What helps harness the 'butterfly effect' for the reader is technique and structure, both of which have grounding qualities. This concept may also enable you to gain a greater understanding as to why Spirit can see no difference between action and intent.

27. The Chapter Not To Skip - Business Sense

Being a gifted psychic doesn't mean you will succeed in a very competitive arena as a professional reader. Your success is just as dependent upon your ability to run a business as it is on providing a well-structured, accurate, non-predictive reading.

A Business Plan

Before you become an independent psychic and start your business, it is wise to do a business plan. A business plan will expose all the problems that are avoidable before you start, thus enabling you to avoid costly learning curves. It can also give guidance as to where you start and help you clearly define your goals.

If you plan to be an agency psychic, you still need to consider doing an organisational plan to cater for your work activities outside of the agency. Obviously, it isn't as essential as it would be for an independent.

The Law in Britain

As already mentioned, in April 2008 the Fraudulent Mediums Act 1951 was repealed and replaced by the laws that govern trading standards. This means it is against the law for psychics, professional or otherwise, to predict. For further information on this, I suggest you log onto the SWA website. It is therefore essential that on any advert or website you have "For Entertainment Purposes Only". Other countries may well have different laws, but it is always worth bearing in mind that prediction can and does cause a lot of problems which contribute toward a person ruining his or her life.

For Entertainment Purposes Only

You may well feel indignant that psychics have been allocated under this sector of the market. On the surface of it, this allocation negates the important role psychics have to play within the social structure of society. It may also shows how ignorant society as a whole is with regard to metaphysics.

The wealth of positives to be gained from such an allocation well outstrip any perceived challenges. The allocation has also opened up a sector of the market that knows few boundaries – entertainment – and by doing so promotes psychics, albeit by default, in a manner that none of us could afford if wew were paying a marketing PR agent to achieve the same goal.

A good example of this is Mystic Meg, the trade name for Margaret Lake, who took the country by storm when she was chosen to host the lottery in 1994. It would appear that her appearance hit a subliminal note within the general public. That note triggered our long lost memories of a time when the fortune-teller, the astrologer, the oracle and the psychic played an important role within society. Mystic Meg was the beginning of a massive upsurge in all things psychic. As a result, the demands for the psychic increased thus placing our profession in the spotlight, where it still remains today.

The 'powers that be' had unwittingly let the proverbial genie out of the bottle, and it is still free. This is an excellent example of the hand of Spirit at work.

Insurance

Like all professionally run businesses you need insurance. Those who decide to opt for going on a course should be covered by the course. Check to make sure you are insured and keep it up when you graduate.

The fact that you may also be a qualified and practicing comple-mentary health therapist doesn't mean you are automatically insured for psychic readings. BAPS[10] and the SWA provide very good policies.

For insurance purposes, many insurance companies still place the profession of a psychic, medium and tarot reader under that of 'Entertainment'.

Running a Business

The business 'tools of the trade' for both agency and independent psychics are a line telephone, a diary and, if necessary, a computer.

As an independent, you will also need a portable credit card machine, a PDQ, to take credit or debit card payments. If you have a web site you will need an ePDQ system such as Paypal and Sagepay, which may be cheaper than the banks systems. Both a business bank account and a merchant account are necessary to process the payments you receive. You will also need a good and reliable telecommunications company to provide and manage a premium rate number (PRN) such as an 0906 number. They cost in the region of £45.00 – 55.00 at the time of writing. Not having a 0906 number, you can expect to lose a lot of money.

If you adopt the relevant tried and tested business practices already in place, the likelihood of you succeeding increases. Good business practice is to first recognise that you are a business, and being responsible for it provides you with a solid foundation from which you can then build your business. A solid foundation starts with you understanding what is involved in being self-employed and running a small business.

If you haven't established a good foundation before you start trading, the consequences may well catch up with you

---

10 British Astrological and Psychics Soc. http://www.baps.uk.com

when you least expect it and you could find it impossible to function efficiently, which will affect the quality of your readings. Long term, it will stop you from reaching your full potential both as a reader and when conducting yourself in a businesslike manner.

Therefore, from day one it is wise to start keeping records, which need to include the names, addresses and telephone numbers of your clients. This is essential if you wish to cover yourself against any untrue and unfounded accusations or otherwise. Keeping records of other people's details takes you into the realms of the Data Protection Act. Make sure your system adheres to that law.

Also, remember to submit yearly accounts on time and pay for your advertising, National Insurance contributions and tax bills – these are a must. Here are some basic pointers for you to consider:

- Think Ahead: The market is never static. It is therefore wise to keep an eye on it as well as the sector within which you are working. Always bear in mind that professional psychics fall within the discretionary payment sector. In other words, people cut back on spending within this field when money is tight. That means you may face a fall in calls and therefore income. By anticipating change you are prepared for market fluctuations.
- Keep up with new technology: We live in a technical age and there is no escaping this. If you don't take advantage of this technology, you will severely limit your business income.
- Identify your customer base. This is achieved by knowing your area of expertise.
- Be a partner to your customers: Put yourself in your client's shoes and then ask yourself what you would expect from a reading.
- Update your business plan regularly: How often you do this is dependent upon the financial market. Keeping a

'clients list' can provide you with a wealth of information that will enable you to do this.

- Keep your outgoings to a minimum: Unless you are doing person-to-person readings, you don't need a fancy room - only an area in the house where it is quiet and somewhere for a filing cabinet and a computer.
- Income tax: seek professional advice such as a book keeper or accountant. A good one pays for him- or herself by reducing your tax bill.

Primary Point of Contact with Customers

This is a business term used to explain how you answer the phone or greet a person-to-person client. Telephone greetings say a great deal about your business. A good business is built on good commun-ications. Here are some pointers for those who haven't had any experience in this field:

- Ensure your home environment is organized so that no children, pets, TV or radio can be heard in the background when you are doing a reading.
- Without rushing, answer the phone before the third ring, but don't sound breathless. Carrying a cordless phone in your pocket will help you achieve this.
- When answering the phone, be grounded and focused. Remember your voice at the end of the telephone line is the first impression of you that your caller will get, therefore it needs to sound both friendly and confident.
- If using a trading name, always answer the phone with that name. Your friends will understand.
- Interact with the caller in a clear, courteous but informed manner that will immediately identify who you are. E.g. "Good morning, this is .... speaking. How may I help you?" Over-familiarization may put off potential customers.
- Have pen and paper close to hand.

- Give the information when required - which usually centres around fees, length of the reading, how you read and when you are available.
- Avoid falling into the trap of giving a free reading, which comes under the guise of a person asking for proof that you are a 'proper' psychic, before they decide to pay for a reading.
- Don't allow people to waste your time.
- Take payment in advance if a proposed client phones to make an appointment. A lot of people say they will phone back at an appointed time and then don't. This means you have lost business when it was avoidable.

Advertising, Marketing and Promoting for Independent Psychics

If you do not advertise, no one knows you exist. Advertising in the right places, which are dedicated national magazines, can be expensive. If the advert isn't clear, catchy and precise or if it isn't being shown in the appropriate outlets, you will get very little, custom, if any . The money you do spend will be money down the drain.

Enter the advertising in stages, one dedicated magazine at a time and booking the advert for a year, making sure you pay monthly. This way you will get a better rate.

The only way you will find your advertising niche is through trial and error. If you do not monitor the traffic from your adverts you do not know how it is performing. If an advert doesn't pay for itself and show a profit, look at the design of the advert.

Consider cancelling the adverts in the magazines that are no longer paying for themselves in a continuous three month period, that doesn't include the summer holiday months of June, July and August. It takes about two months before you know if a new advert will bear fruit. Once you start to receive an income over and above the cost of the advert, consider taking out another advert in another magazine.

You don't necessarily need a web site to take advantage of web advertising. Being a member of an organisation such as BAPS means your details will be listed on their web site.

If you opt for a web site, you can get immediate results from Google Adwords, Yahoo and Just Ask etc., - but don't fall into the trap of thinking you have to pay top click price to get a response. The general public have wised up to the fact that the psychic agencies are on the front pages and independents behind them. Those who do not want an agency reading will take the time to seek you out.

Be aware that there are some web-advertising agencies that claim they can get your advert to the top of the first page of the search engines. You could lose a lot of money going down this path.

It is important to think of advertising, marketing and promotion together - what makes sense for advertising may not be wise from the promotion angle. It doesn't look professional if you put a handwritten card up in the news-agents.

Because advertising is expensive, a lot of psychics only advertise locally. To deal with the local side of advertising, you should find respected and established magazines like Green Events or the Connection Magazine, both of which are still in circulation at the time of writing.

28. Finding Work - Agency vs. Independent

Although many think otherwise, there is no difference in the quality of work between psychics who work for an agency and those who are independent.

Pros and Cons of Agency Work

The benefit of starting off with agency work is that it provides you with a basic structure until you have developed your own structure and technique. It also helps you to gain your confidence.

Agency work is convenient and flexible because you can log on and off when it suits you and the agency. Although you can earn good money working with a successful agency, the down side is it will probably be less than what you would earn working as an established independent. Being self-employed you are still responsible for your taxes and national insurance. The agency is not liable unless it says otherwise in the contract.

If you are happy with an agency, there is no reason why you can't stay with them year in, year out. Many gifted psychics do this because it suits them to do so.

If it is your goal to be an independent reader then choose an agency name and keep your trading name, the name you wish to be known as, for when you work as an independent.

Seeking Employment with a Psychic Agency

All agencies prefer psychics with practical experience. Therefore, when starting out, approach the smaller psychic agencies first because they may be easier to join rather than the leading ones. The benefit of joining a smaller agency first is that you can gain experience at a professional level. You may not get as much money, but you are getting paid to finish off your training.

If you wish to change agencies due to lack of work or money, you let the larger agency know this, but you do not have to let them know which agency you are working for or go into details.

Approaching an Agency

An agency will probably ask if you are already working within in the field or for another agency. This is where your practice readings come into it's own since you will be able to say "yes".

- How much do I get paid per minute? Don't accept anything less than between £0.25p - £0.30p per minute.
- Am I able to choose when I work? All agencies use a time-formatted rota, which means there will be slots of times for when you can work. The length of time of each slot will vary from agency to agency. You should have an option to change your placement on the rota.
- How long are the time slots and how many slots can they offer you in one day? Try to arrange it so that you don't work any more than four hours in a single slot. If you want to work more than one four- hour slot with a busy agency, do so but have a good break in-between. Do not under-estimate how tiring it can be to wait for calls even though you will be utilizing the time doing something else.
- How many calls would you expect to receive in one slot should you be successful? The answer to this will be that it

will depend upon how good you are as a psychic and how many regulars you attract. But you still need to have an idea.

- Do they contact you requesting you to work additional hours?
- Are you allocated a logging on and off facility?
- When and how do you get paid?

How to Prepare for a Psychic Telephone Reading Test

Always remember, good reputable agencies know what they are doing. They have had years of experience handling both psychics and clients. If an agency needs readers at the time of your call, they will arrange a time for you to do a verbal test reading for them, the length of which could be 20 or 30 minutes and in some cases longer. If not, ask them to put you on their list to contact you when they do need more psychics.

On the day of the test reading, be prepared. That means keeping your clock and keywords next to you, grounding yourself before the reading, and staying grounded throughout the reading. Before starting the reading, view the person you are going to read for as a client not an examiner. He or she is a person too and will be just as interested in what you bring forward through the reading for themselves, as well as determining whether your abilities are to the standard they need.

If you are turned down, without going onto the defensive, ask why the agency does not consider you are up to a professional standard, and practice in those areas. Apply again when you feel it is appropriate as well as applying to other agencies.

If you do not succeed first time, avoid taking it personally. You are going through an invaluable experience that will make all the difference in you succeeding in your goal, which is to become a professional psychic. However, you will only benefi from this if you can see a refusal as a positive, either the agency is not for you or they are identifying you have not yet reached a professional standard and more work is needed. Either which way you cannot lose.

If your reading comes up to standard they should send you a contract.

When Successful

Avoid being pressured to start work without first receiving and reading and signing the contract - also, remember the small print. If you are naturally independent or are already self-employed, there may well come a time when you should prepare to become an independent psychic. The signs for this usually take the form of the agency becoming dissatisfied with your work, or you becoming disenchanted with the agency, or both.

Should this occur, it isn't because you are a bad reader or have suddenly lost the plot - it is because your technique has outgrown that of the reading policies of the agency. It is Spirit's way of showing you that you are a good reader and it's time for you to consider becoming an independent.

The Pros and Cons of Becoming an Independent Psychic

The main advantages of being an independent are:

- Having the freedom to develop your reading methods and not be restricted by agency policy.
- You don't have to contend with the principle 'the client is always right', when hand-on-heart you know that it is not the case.
- You can maintain control of the reading without being concerned that you will receive a telephone call from an agency line manager regarding a customer complaint.
- You can make decisions as to whether you wish to read for someone or not, and when to take a call or not.

204

- You can make more money in less time.

The challenges are:

- If you allow it, you can end up being on call 24/7 so from day one, make sure this doesn't happen.
- It can be restricting unless you make it clear when you are and are not working.
- You are responsible for promoting, marketing and advertising your business.

Person-to-person vs. Telephone Readings

Person-to-person readings are when you meet the client face-to-face. This applies only to those psychics who are independent. There is no difference in quality of work between psychics who do person-to-person and those who do telephone readings; it is up to an individual psychic's and client's preference.

You can accommodate both ways of working if you so wish. Some psychics are more comfortable meeting their clients, others not. From the business perspective, if you decide not to do phone readings, you run the risk of reducing your income between 30 - 50%.

Person-to-person

The majority of people who seek person-to-person readings are law-abiding citizens. Never the less common sense demands you put your safety first and belongings second when meeting a stranger in your own home.

The length of a person-to-person reading usually takes longer than when held over the phone. Obviously, this needs to be borne in mind when setting your fees. When working from home, unless you know the person, always process the payment before starting the reading.

If travelling to your client, remember to add on travelling expenses and always ask for a deposit, which needs to have been cleared by your bank the day before you travel. It is always wise to ask for the balance before the reading starts.

Telephone Readings

Telephone readings are when you conduct the reading over the telephone rather than meeting clients face-to-face. There is a misguided notion that telephone readings are not as good as person-to-person. This is not the case. They provide the client with a degree of anonymity and a psychic distance, which reinforces his or her boundaries. Telephone reading work falls into two categories - agency and independent. The two don't mix unless you have two reading names.

- Agency Work: As already discussed, working for an agency is the simplest form of telephone work. You log on when you have arranged to do so and then log off at the right time. You can do it as a part time job or as a career.
- Independent Work: See under 'Running a Business'

The Transition from Agency to Independent

Being self-employed, you legally have the right to be an independent and work for an agency at the same time. Nevertheless, you need to check your contract with the agency. If an agency gets wind that you are working as an independent whilst on their books, they may or may not raise the issue with you and probably find a reason to dismiss you. If you leave an agency before becoming an independent you will lose money.

To avoid this, before you advise the agency of your intentions to become an independent, advertise in dedicated spiritual national magazines using your trading name. This will give you the anonymity you need.

When you are earning enough as an independent, you can then leave the agency.

29. Being a Professional Psychic

It takes confidence in yourself to be a professional psychic. Confidence is derived from a protocol that becomes part of the technique and structure of your reading. Keeping to a protocol enables you to hit the ground running and includes:

Confidentiality

Your client will expect you to keep all the information that comes through a reading confidential. This means that you should not share the content of a reading with anyone else without the client's permission.

Even so, you will find that some clients will phone because concerned about a relative, friend or loved one. This is a very natural and understandable thing to do, but it does raise the issue of third party confidentiality. Unless the client is being directly affected by, and is involved in the persons' situation, the psychic should not release any information. If the person is directly involved it can only be released around what they are directly involved in.

Therefore, you need to explain that you have not received permission from the person your client is enquiring about to release such information. You can ask if they have received permission to ask for such information and if 'yes' you can consider going ahead,

Morals and Ethics

Your priority is to do no harm - directly, indirectly or by default. You achieve this by knowing your limitations and working within those parameters. Here are some more pointers to consider:

- Avoid becoming embroiled in legal, financial or medical matters if you are not trained to do so. Refer your client to the Citizens Advice Bureau or have a list of organisations or phone numbers for relevant governing bodies to give out.
- Maintain your boundaries at all times by keeping your emotions in check. When your emotions are in check, you are grounded.
- Remember that your client is paying you for a service and expects value for money.
- Never accept any abuse from a client.
- Keep your temper in check by stopping the reading before it deteriorates into an argument.
- If you feel the client isn't happy but isn't saying anything, raise the issue.
  - Use your common sense.
- Avoid using the reading to sell something, unless you know it can assist.
- Do not allow yourself to be put off-course if and when a client tells you they have reeived different information from another psychic.

Comfort Readings

A comfort reading is when a psychic tells the client what he or she wants to hear even though the messages they receive oppose that 'want'. Other reasons why comfort readings occur, are because the psychic doesn't wish to be:

- Shouted at.
- Challenged.

- Told he or she is wrong.
- Told that other psychics have said everything will work out for the best, (and now you know why).
- Responsible for a client bursting into tears.

Therefore it is the reader's issues that cause comfort readings.

It is not easy to pass messages from Spirit that are contrary to the client's expectations, and it needs to be done with sensitivity.

Nor is it morally or ethically acceptable for a psychic to edit out or change the messages coming through from Spirit. Editing out isn't usually done consciously, but the end result is that the client isn't aware of the true situation. This misleads the client and usually prolongs their agony.

The vast majority of clients want to hear the truth of the matter despite the fact that they are hoping to hear that everything is going to work out and not to worry. They have an inner knowing of the true nature of their situation before they phone a psychic; it may not be a conscious knowing, never the less it is there. This knowing gives the client the strength they need to hear messages that the psychic may find hard to deliver.

Timing the Readings

When it comes to credit or debit card readings, it is up to you to decide how long you wish to read for a client. Irrespective of the length of time, it should be universal for all clients so everyone knows where they stand. When making this decision you need to bear in mind the following:

- Your energy levels.
- The clients' attention span.

The rule of thumb is quantity isn't quality. It doesn't usually take more than thirty minutes to deal with a client's issues. If you feel more confident doing a longer reading, do so, but make sure your charges reflect the additional time. You can extend the reading when is deemed necessary by the client and charge for the additional time.

There is always the option to provide choice - a longer or shorter reading - and the fees are adjusted accordingly. The PRN can't be any more than 20 minutes, so there is no decision to make.

Overruns

An overrun is when a reading runs over the allotted time. There are two reasons for this. Firstly you have allowed it; secondly the situation demanded an extension. Overruns are controlled with self-discipline and organisation since it is your responsibility to make sure you don't go over the allotted time.

Most clients don't keep a note of the time, but a few will and some will argue that you haven't gone the full term of the reading when you have. Using a telephone that displays the timing of the call for telephone readings assists greatly, since a client can bring the timing of your clock or wristwatch into question. A person-to-person reading is easier because you can synchronise watches before you start.

On occasion a client will deliberately try to extend the reading by saying "I know we are nearly finished (when in fact you have just started your closing statement), but can I ask one more question?" Unless a regular client, your answer is "no, we have come to the end of the reading", or "we can extend the reading but it will cost you a further ..."

When the situation demands it, the choice is yours, you either ask the client if they wish to extend and take additional payment, or offer your services free, but let the client know this.

Tears

If your advert and introduction are a true reflection of how you work, clients will be forewarned as to what they can expect. Most clients do not get emotional during a reading, but some do and with cause. Again, you need a policy to handle such occasions - otherwise a comfort reading develops by default.

If your reading technique and structure are in place then you should be able to stop, for no more than a couple of seconds. This will allow the client to shed a tear or two and then carry on with the reading after enquiring if the client is ready to do so. Speaking with a softened but still strong, secure and confident tone, make sure you keep a check on your own emotions at the same time by closing your heart chakra.

Empathy and Sympathy

Spirit is at work whilst a person is in the process of choosing a psychic reader. Since there are no coincidences, there will always be a reason why you were chosen. This means that time and again you will find yourself in a position where you have gone through or are going through an eerily similar situation to that of your client.

At such times, please remember that the reading is about your client and not you. Your client doesn't want to hear about you and your problems.

Clients are also psychic and some will be practising or professional. They will pick up that you have gone through something similar, without you, saying very little, if anything at all. This is because you will be giving them the understanding that can only come from one who has gone through something similar.

Dependency

Phoning psychics can become addictive. It is really important that you have a policy in place that prevents dependency from developing. The rule of thumb is one reading per week unless there is a crisis unfolding. During crises, no more than one full reading or two short readings (adjust your fees accordingly), per day, reverting back to once a week when YOU feel it is appropriate. Do not rely on the client to make this decision, although many do without any problem.

Frauds and Con Artists who Pose as Clients

Ninety-five percent of your clients are honest individuals. The other five percent may not be and will attempt to get a free reading from you by:

- Phoning up the credit/debit card telephone number pretending they have phoned the 0906 PRN. Make sure your service provider puts a 'whisper' on your 0906 number, which identifies when you are receiving a PRN call. Otherwise you will lose a lot of money.
- A proposed client uses another person's credit/debit card. You cannot accept payment even if the legal owner of the card has given permission, since they can withdraw it after the reading.
- A person uses another family member's credit/debit card without first asking their permission and doesn't tell you it isn't their card.
- If you accept payment by cheque, arrange for the reading after the cheque has cleared.

No one is Perfect

There are no hard or fast rules as to how to be a good and successful professional psychic. It comes with hard work, commitment using your common sense and being prepared to learn on the job.

The marker for you to know how well you are doing is obviously related to how much money you make. However, you also need to make a note of how many return calls and referrals you get. If you don't get any, you need to stop, take a recording of a reading you do and listen to it. Unless you ue a telephone system that records the full conversation, you don't need to ask your client's permission. Then make the necessary changes to your technique and structure.

No one is perfect, so you must not be too hard on yourself if you feel annoyed or frustrated at times during or after a reading. If you do find yourself becoming annoyed on line, what is important is how you handle the situation. A 'hands-up' approach is always best rather than attempting to put the onus on the client or provide an excuse.

Sometimes Spirit uses those very emotions to enable a client to pick up on the message. It happens to all professional psychics and shows that you are caring and being conscientious. As long as you harness those emotions as much as you can during the reading, you are doing your best and no one can ask more from you than that.

Even so, do what you can to make sure such an incident happens rarely. By that I mean no more than maybe three times a year, judging by an average of five readings a day for an independent and more if working for an agency. If you exceed this number of incidents, it can mean you could be starting to show signs of suffering from burnout and it is time for you to take a break or reduce the number of readings you do each day for a while.

Some psychics find that some days they just cannot make a connection with their clients. Usually you are not aware that it's one of those days until you have done a reading that goes pear-shaped. This being the case - close down the reading, give a refund if necessary, and get off the lines immediately, have a cup of tea and ground yourself.

Keep to the policy that you never read when you are ill or over-stressed.

The Road to Hell

No one becomes a psychic with the intention of doing anyone harm, quite the opposite. There is an idiom, 'The road to hell is paved with good intensions' and it couldn't be truer than with this profession.

Well-meaning psychics trying to 'help' their client have often caused a lot of harm. This means the psychics boundaries were not in place and therefore there could be no technique or structure to the reading.

Working out a strategy that deals with all the issues mentioned above can provide you with a platform that can enable you to present yourself as a professional psychic, as long as you remember to keep to the protocol.

The Modern Day Agony Aunt or Uncle

The fact is, whether you wish it or not, by working as a professional psychic you are also setting yourself up as a person someone can turn to when they feel there is no-one else.

From the minute you answer the phone, you need to place your client in a position of security, where they are safe in the knowledge that they know they can share with you their innermost secrets, desires and fears.

The ramifications of this are that you have also taken on the roles of counsellor and agony aunt or uncle as well as a psychic. If you are already a qualified counsellor you will be able to take this in your stride. If not, consider going on a counselling course, or suggest your client goes to counselling if you think it is appropriate. Please do not underestimate the responsibilities involved in dealing with another person's problems and not being qualified to do so.

Spirit is Ready When You Are

There are a lot of incredibly gifted, intelligent psychics who stop short of becoming professional. This is because making that initial telephone enquiry to the agency or the thought of starting out as an independent is challenging. Most professional psychics will have gone through the process of knowing they should apply to one of the agencies, but they do a very good job convincing themselves that they aren't ready, or it's 'not the right time' - that excuse is a favourite.

As a consequence, most professional psychics were driven onto the lines due to financial hardship. This doesn't mean they were and are selling their souls for money, it means they are being driven by Spirit to help themselves on a practical level by walking the path of a professional psychic.

Others will have been drawn to the profession not due to financial hardship but due to the quality of their lifestyle, or lack of it. Then there are those who could make sense of their lives in no other way. Only a few end up as professional psychics because it was their chosen career. Always bear in mind, Spirit helps those who help themselves. Don't deny that help because it is coming through your spiritual wealth.

There is nothing stopping you from transforming your spiritual wealth in to financial wealth other than yourself, so get yourself out of the way.

Appendix 1
Elizabeth Francis
Keywords for Tarot

The Minor Arcana

No.	Numerology Aspect	Wands – Fire	Cups – Water	Swords – Air	Disks – Earth
		Enterprise, Work Business Success Personal Development	Emotions Relationship with Self & Others Healing	Problems Strength Psychic Ability Solutions Thinking	Materialism, Money Practicalities Spiritual and Financial Wealth Rewards
		Fiery, energetic, warm, impulsive, creative, career generous, male aspect, action	Passive, flow, the subconscious, secretive, dreamy, artistic, female aspect, receptive	Logical, space, communication, discrimination, analytical, problems	Traditional, skilful, secure, stable, building solid, the conscious, the shallow planes.
Ace	The essence, pure energy, not yet conscious thought.	New job opportunities may be coming up, New start/ Take stock	New relationship coming into the offing. Good health / Egotistical	New problems forming / Developing the strength to handle a situation	Pay rise in the offing, buying a property, moving, inheritance / False financial security.
2	Union, producing, manifesta-tion	Signs of achievement / Foundation new being laid	Understanding & love / Arguments	Undecided / Care is needed when deciding. Decisions.	Juggling, potential more organization needed / Plans may not work out. Wait before spending.

No.	Numerology Aspect	Wands – Fire	Cups – Water	Swords – Air	Disks – Earth
3	Creating discipline, the result of union (ace + two). Last stage of conscious thought	Assistance available partnership/ Talents being wasted, a new direction.	Happy conclusion, new lifestyle/ What was good is now causing pain – change necessary.	Heartache and disappointment/ Situation not so severe	Great skill, abilities or talent/ Insufficient experience, wasting natural talent.
4	Building, stable establishing, organised.	Harmony peace, satisfaction / More improvement.	Discontent, boredom / New relationship.	New plans, isolated/ Good opportunities.	Materialism/ attached to materialism. Loss, obstacles.
5	Breaking down, evolving, stress, change, conflict.	Agitation, struggle/ Harmony will prevail.	Confusion / Things looking better.	Lack of sensitivity/ No change, loss can be incurred.	Time to review what you want / Karmic lesson: understand burdens.
6	Harmony, beauty, success at a price, self–created problems.	Having faith / Unable to get it together.	Meet old friend / Rewards, recognition may be delayed.	Difficult cycle coming to an end/ Stand back and wait, but not for long.	Enjoy fruits of labour/ Unsatisfactory situation.

No.	Numerology Aspect.	Wands – Fire	Cups – Water	Swords – Air	Disks – Earth	
7	Vision of next situation, cycles of nature, magical number.	Inner strength / Find your strength to clear the tables to start again.	Unable to decide / On the right track on an emotional level.	Things may not work out as planned / Held responsible.	Change for the better / Anxiety about finances.	
8	Fate, reaping what has been sown.	Movement, news coming / Insecurity.	Unsatisfied / Interests lie in material pleasure.	Have experienced hurt, anxiety / Things getting better.	Stable and prepared / Going about things the 'wrong' way to balance Karma	
9	Sociability, extending into the world. Nearly finished.	Maintain control, forthcoming venture / Lack of initiative	Wish come true / Wish not fulfilled, you get what you need not what you want.	Despair, hopelessness / New hope soon.	Still seeking although successful / Time to analyze your desires.	
10	End of cycle Leading to new beginnings.	Under pressure / Talent, skills gained the hard way.	Happiness obtained / Depression, sadness.	Death card, end of a cycle, nothing to be done / Better days.	Feeling secure / Nothing running smoothly, time to move on & drop baggage.	

The Court Cards

Card names, representations and related Zodiac signs.	Wands – Fire	Cups – Water	Swords – Air	Disks – Earth	
	Work energy, business success, enterprise and distinction. Indicates movement, activity, travel and change.	Emotions, psychic ability, love, happiness, loved ones, deep emotions and concerns.	Strength, thinking, indicates problems, pressures, concerns, struggle, effort and endeavour.	Materialism, practicalities, common sense, grounded. A tendency to get stuck in a rut.	
King Male, father. Taurus, Leo, Scorpio Aquarius.	Moving, strong energy, more lasting than the Prince card.	Reliable, respected, trustworthy, from any walk of life, can assist you.	Has authority, could be with the government or associated with law. Gives excellent counsel.	Good position in industry, generous, affectionate and materialistic, easily lead.	
Queen Female, mother. Aries, Cancer, Libra, Capricorn.	Female with an attractive personality and the ability to draw people to her.	Sensitive lady who relies on her intuitive ability more than common sense. Passive, finds assertion hard, gives in.	Lady with sharp wit who appears to have money. Has an interesting, but difficult history.	A creative lady with many talents, family oriented and charitable. Insecure, suspicious.	

Prince Young male, brother, son, nephew. Gemini, Virgo, Sagittarius, Pisces.	Creates change and sudden decisions Conscious, activating energy, not long lasting insecure. Tends to have to have his own way and is controlling.	Can offer interesting invitations or proposals. Good female side. Holds the Holy Spirit energy. Immature.	Courteous young man, good intentions but over bearing attitude. Thinks before he acts and has a tendency to play games.	Thorough and will take the time to do a good job. Can be slow or even stop, finds it hard to get started again. Can be irresponsible and impatient.
Princess Young female, sister, niece, cousin.	Indication of message from a relative or friend. Practical, has a natural understanding of the everyday expressions of the elements.	Can offer help or co-operate, gentle and quiet. Nirvana. May also represent a young man with an active female side.	Activities of this person can cause you concern. Unpredictable, prepare for the unexpected.	Enjoys studying and scholarly, quiet and moody but goal oriented.

The Major Arcana		
0	THE FOOL	Impetuous, youthful, follows hopes / New enterprise, courage to go where angels dare to tread / Decisions, crossroads, think carefully, worldly values drag back.
1	MAGICIAN	New abilities, working with the elements, transmitter and transmitted, illusion, communication, can create something out of nothing / Abuse of power, manipulation.
2	HIGH PRIESTESS	Intuition, balance, wisdom, activity beneath the surface, much depth / A tendency to be deceitful and calculating, abusing the knowledge of wisdom.
3	EMPRESS	Fruitfulness, creativity, growth, pregnancy, assertion of the female energy. / Restricting growth and female intuition co-dependency upon a male energy.
4	EMPEROR	Authority, logic, reason, knowledge, experience stability / Martial qualities, shortlived energies, dominant and controlling male energy.
5	HIEROPHANT	Bridge, guidance, advice, teacher, foundation, self-control / Lessons to be learned before moving on.
6	LOVERS	Choice of paths, choice of direction, soul-mate / The need to form a relationship with oneself before being able to form a relationship with another.
7	CHARIOT	Individual direction, integration, perfect control, self discipline, triumphant / Tendency to be a control freak.
8	JUSTICE	Judgment based on truth of situation, fate, reward, achieving balance / Recognizing learning curves and implementing them.
9	HERMIT	Reliance on own inner strength, teacher, fertility, courage to face inner-self, courage to stand alone / Isolation, acute loneliness.

10	WHEEL OF FORTUNE	Karma, cause and effect, new cycle, fruits of what you have put into your life / Balancing Karma and slowing down the Karmic Wheel by recognizing 'you have been there before' and using the experience to avoid further cause and effect.
11	STRENGTH	Inherent strength, curbing and restraining instincts / Gentleness, diplomacy.
12	HANGED MAN	Looking at things from a different perspective. Action suspended, ability to change, a test, illusion.
13	DEATH	Transformation, change, new situation / Need to let go, painful emotions.
14	TEMPERANCE	Balance and transmutation, Inner balance, harmony, rebirth, integration / Be careful, slow down.
15	DEVIL	Wrapped up in materialism, off course, wants that chain us and stop our progress / Raising our lowering of the Male.
16	TOWER	Sudden shattering of ideals and false concepts, destruction of ego, power of sound / Clearing the tables to start again, positive, not negative.
17	STAR	New opportunities, widening horizons, emotions / Need to be understood. Day dreamer
18	MOON	Intuition, faith, fears, lonely, testing time, dreams, sleep, female energy, working with what is hidden / Deception, misunderstanding.
19	SUN	Integration, wholeness, success, life / realistic, Egotistical, bully.
20	JUDGMENT	Vocation, rebirth, detachment, choice, good things, becoming balanced / Lonely, uneasy, trapped, becoming unbalanced.
21	WORLD	Integrated, successful, completion of cycle / Fear of new ideas, static.

The above Key is to be used as guidelines only.

Appendix 2

Density 1 is the heaviest density 14 is the lightest.

Table VI
Correspondence of Dimensions and Levels
and their Psychic Definitions

Identity Level	Dimension	Correlation	Psychic Definition
0	0	The parallel dimension to the Zero and right angle the 1st dimension.	The point. Pre-birth of Pure thought form. Flat. Inert Dimensionless, gateway to the inter-dimensions. What isn't in the dimensions.
1 Incarnate Subconscious Mind	1st Dimension Atomic Body	A parallel dimension and right angle to Zero and the 2nd dimension	Spatial – Length Movement Birth of thought forms
1 Incarnate Emotional/ Instinctual Mind	2nd Dimension Emotional Body	A parallel dimension and right angle to the 1st and 4th dimensions.	Spatial - Structure 1. Left/Right 2. Up/Down The forming of thought forms and the mind

1 Reasoning Mind	3rd Dimension Mental Body	A parallel dimension and right angle to the 1st, 2nd, 6th and 9th dimensions.	Spatial - Space 1. Left/Right 2.Back/Forth _3. Up/Down The completion of thought forms and the mind
2 Soul The Astral Mind	4th Dimension	A parallel dimension and right angle to the 2nd and 8th dimensions.	Time and anti-time – Direction straight and perpendicular. Left/Right _2. Back/Forth _3. Up/Down Flight and the manifestation of thought forms through the mind
2 Soul The Archetypal Mind	5th Dimension	A parallel dimension and right angle. Dimension to 2nd, 3rd and the 10th dimensions.	Unification. Quantum Concept. Transcending the speed of light. Mind over matter. The forming of alternate realities through decision-making.
2 Soul The Angelic Mind	6th Dimension	A parallel and right angle. Dimension to the 3rd and 12th dimensions.	Direction. The 1st Gateway to alternative realities formed by our decision process and their conclusion. The realities that are not open to us. The portal out of the governing matrix.
3 Oversoul The Ketheric Mind	7th Dimension	A parallel and right angle. Dimension to the 2nd, 5th and 14th dimensions.	Gateway to Pure Thought Form. Enlightenment. The sum total of dimensions dot to 6.
3 Oversoul The Monadic Mind	8th Dimension The Meta- Galactic Core	A parallel and right angle dimension of the 4th and 16th dimensions	Holds and provides access to the past and future in matter-less form. Infinity.

3 Oversoul The Keriatic Mind	9th Dimension The Galactic Core	A parallel and right angle dimension to 18th dimension	Holds the continual present outside of time in matter-less form. The Causal Mind, the Planetary Mind Matrix
4 The Avatar Self-divinity the decent of a deity	10th Dimension The Christiac Mind	A parallel and right angle dimension to the 5th and 20th dimension	Vibration The formation of multi- universes and the omni- universe from matter-less thought form
4 The Avatar Self-divinity The decent of a deity in the embodiment of self	11th Dimension The Buddhiac Mind	A parallel and right angle dimension to the 5th, 6th and 22nd dimensions	The 2nd Gateway Unification of the Collective and the hyper- communication
4 The Avatar Self-divinity The decent of deity and the personification of self	12th Dimension The Nirvnic Mind	A parallel and right angle dimension to the 3rd 6th 9th and 24th dimensions	The Solar Matrix is a part of the multi dimensional identity
5 Rishi (M) Riskika (F) Combined	13th Dimension	A parallel and right angle dimension to the 1st, 6th 7th 12th and 26th dimensions	Time Matrix – Universal manifestation templates within the Cosmic Energy Matrix. Within the time matrix the 15 dimensions are arranged into three sets of dimensions forming the five 3 dimensional reality field called the Harmonic Universe.

5 Rishi (M) Riskika (F) Combined		A parallel and right angle dimension to the 7th and 28th Dimensions	
	14th Dimension		The Energy Matrix – The Cosmic Manifestation Template Primal Sound Fields and their Primal Tonal-vibrational Life Force Currents
5 Rishi (M) Riskika (F) Combined	15th Dimension	A parallel and right angle dimension to the 1st, 7th 8rd and the 30th Dimensions	

Appendix 3

Answers to earlier questions posed:
- Do you see things out the corner of your eye, in your peripheral vision, such as movement, lights or shadows? If yes, you are a peripheral clairvoyant.

- Can you picture an apple or a colour that represents an apple, in your head? If yes, you are a third eye clairvoyant.

- Do you see colours around people, or see the deceased or images that others cannot see? If yes, you are visually clairvoyant.

- Can you walk into a room and pick up on an atmosphere or sit in a chair and have to move because you are not comfortable? If yes, you are clairsentient.

- Do you get unassociated thoughts coming across your head, and you think, "What did I think that for?" If yes, you are clairaudient.

- Are you 'light sensitive'? The more 'light sensitive' you are the more you are able to read what is happening within the planes of existence.

- Do you think of someone and then meet him or her, or they phone? If yes, you have ESP ability (extra sensory perception).

- Do your dreams sometimes provide information? If yes, you are a dream worker.

- Do you dream or think of vents that occur a few days or months later? If yes, you are precognitive.

- Can you smell aromas that you know cannot be caused by anything in your house? If yes, you are Clairalient.

- Do you get different tastes in your mouth, (and you do not suffer from a medical condition that would cause this anomaly)? If yes, you are Clairgustant

- Do you know things without being taught? If yes, you are Claircognizant.

FREE DETAILED CATALOGUE

Capall Bann is owned and run by people actively involved in many of the areas in which we publish. A detailed illustrated catalogue is available on request, SAE or International Postal Coupon appreciated. **Titles can be ordered direct from Capall Bann,** by post (cheque or PO with order), via our web site **www.capallbann.co.uk** using credit/debit card or Paypal, or from good bookshops and specialist outlets.

A Breath Behind Time, Terri Hector
A Soul is Born by Eleyna Williamson
Angels and Goddesses - Celtic Christianity & Paganism, M. Howard
The Art of Conversation With the Genius Loci, Barry Patterson
Arthur - The Legend Unveiled, C Johnson & E Lung
Astrology The Inner Eye - A Guide in Everyday Language, E Smith
Auguries and Omens - The Magical Lore of Birds, Yvonne Aburrow
Asyniur - Women's Mysteries in the Northern Tradition, S McGrath
Beginnings - Geomancy, Builder's Rites & Electional Astrology in the
    European Tradition, Nigel Pennick
Between Earth and Sky, Julia Day
The Book of Seidr, Runic John
Caer Sidhe - Celtic Astrology and Astronomy, Michael Bayley
Call of the Horned Piper, Nigel Jackson
Can't Sleep, Won't Sleep, Linda Louisa Dell
Carnival of the Animals, Gregor Lamb
Cat's Company, Ann Walker
Celebrating Nature, Gordon MacLellan
Celtic Faery Shamanism, Catrin James
Celtic Faery Shamanism - The Wisdom of the Otherworld, Catrin James
Celtic Lore & Druidic Ritual, Rhiannon Ryall
Celtic Sacrifice - Pre Christian Ritual & Religion, Marion Pearce
Celtic Saints and the Glastonbury Zodiac, Mary Caine
Circle and the Square, Jack Gale
Come Back To Life, Jenny Smedley
Company of Heaven, Jan McDonald
Compleat Vampyre - The Vampyre Shaman, Nigel Jackson
Cottage Witchcraft, Jan McDonald
Creating Form From the Mist - The Wisdom of Women in Celtic Myth and
    Culture, Lynne Sinclair-Wood
Crystal Clear - A Guide to Quartz Crystal, Jennifer Dent
Crystal Doorways, Simon & Sue Lilly

Crossing the Borderlines - Guising, Masking & Ritual Animal Disguise in the
    European Tradition, Nigel Pennick
Dragons of the West, Nigel Pennick
Dreamtime by Linda Louisa Dell
Dreamweaver by Elen Sentier
Earth Dance - A Year of Pagan Rituals, Jan Brodie
Earth Harmony - Places of Power, Holiness & Healing, Nigel Pennick
Earth Magic, Margaret McArthur
Egyptian Animals - Guardians & Gateways of the Gods, Akkadia Ford
Eildon Tree (The) Romany Language & Lore, Michael Hoadley
Enchanted Forest - The Magical Lore of Trees, Yvonne Aburrow
Eternal Priestess, Sage Weston
Eternally Yours Faithfully, Roy Radford & Evelyn Gregory
Everything You Always Wanted To Know About Your Body, But So Far
    Nobody's Been Able To Tell You, Chris Thomas & D Baker
Experiencing the Green Man, Rob Hardy & Teresa Moorey
Face of the Deep - Healing Body & Soul, Penny Allen
Fairies and Nature Spirits, Teresa Moorey
Fairies in the Irish Tradition, Molly Gowen
Familiars - Animal Powers of Britain, Anna Franklin
Flower Wisdom, Katherine Kear
Fool's First Steps, (The) Chris Thomas
Forest Paths - Tree Divination, Brian Harrison, Ill. S. Rouse
From Past to Future Life, Dr Roger Webber
From Stagecraft To Witchcraft, Patricia Crowther
Gardening For Wildlife Ron Wilson
God Year, The, Nigel Pennick & Helen Field
Goddess on the Cross, Dr George Young
Goddess Year, The, Nigel Pennick & Helen Field
Goddesses, Guardians & Groves, Jack Gale
Handbook For Pagan Healers, Liz Joan
Handbook of Fairies, Ronan Coghlan
Healing Book, The, Chris Thomas and Diane Baker
Healing Homes, Jennifer Dent
Healing Journeys, Paul Williamson
Healing Stones, Sue Philips
Heathen Paths - Viking and Anglo Saxon Beliefs by Pete Jennings
Herb Craft - Shamanic & Ritual Use of Herbs, Lavender & Franklin
Hidden Heritage - Exploring Ancient Essex, Terry Johnson
Hub of the Wheel, Skytoucher
In and Out the Windows, Dilys Gator
In Search of Herne the Hunter, Eric Fitch
In Search of the Green Man, Peter Hill
Inner Celtia, Alan Richardson & David Annwn
Inner Mysteries of the Goths, Nigel Pennick
Inner Space Workbook - Develop Through Tarot, Cat Summers & Julian Vayne

In Search of Pagan Gods, Teresa Moorey
Intuitive Journey, Ann Walker Isis - African Queen, Akkadia Ford
Journey Home, The, Chris Thomas
Kecks, Keddles & Kesh - Celtic Lang & The Cog Almanac, Bayley
Language of the Psycards, Berenice
Legend of Robin Hood, The, Richard Rutherford-Moore
Lid Off the Cauldron, Patricia Crowther
Light From the Shadows - Modern Traditional Witchcraft, Gwyn
Living Tarot, Ann Walker
Lore of the Sacred Horse, Marion Davies
Lost Lands & Sunken Cities (2nd ed.), Nigel Pennick
Lyblác, Anglo Saxon Witchcraft by Wulfeage
The Magic and Mystery of Trees, Teresa Moorey
Magic For the Next 1,000 Years, Jack Gale
Magic of Herbs - A Complete Home Herbal, Rhiannon Ryall
Magical Guardians - Exploring the Spirit and Nature of Trees, Philip Heselton
Magical History of the Horse, Janet Farrar & Virginia Russell
Magical Lore of Animals, Yvonne Aburrow
Magical Lore of Cats, Marion Davies
Magical Lore of Herbs, Marion Davies
The Magical Properties of Plants - and How to Find Them by Tylluan Penry
Magick Without Peers, Ariadne Rainbird & David Rankine
Masks of Misrule - Horned God & His Cult in Europe, Nigel Jackson
Medicine For The Coming Age, Lisa Sand MD
Medium Rare - Reminiscences of a Clairvoyant, Muriel Renard
Menopausal Woman on the Run, Jaki da Costa
Mind Massage - 60 Creative Visualisations, Marlene Maundrill
Mirrors of Magic - Evoking the Spirit of the Dewponds, P Heselton
The Moon and You, Teresa Moorey
Moon Mysteries, Jan Brodie
Mysteries of the Runes, Michael Howard
Mystic Life of Animals, Ann Walker
New Celtic Oracle The, Nigel Pennick & Nigel Jackson
Oracle of Geomancy, Nigel Pennick
Pagan Feasts - Seasonal Food for the 8 Festivals, Franklin & Phillips
Paganism For Teens, Jess Wynne
Patchwork of Magic - Living in a Pagan World, Julia Day
Pathworking - A Practical Book of Guided Meditations, Pete Jennings
Personal Power, Anna Franklin
Pickingill Papers - The Origins of Gardnerian Wicca, Bill Liddell
Pillars of Tubal Cain, Nigel Jackson
Places of Pilgrimage and Healing, Adrian Cooper
Planet Earth - The Universe's Experiment, Chris Thomas
Practical Divining, Richard Foord
Practical Meditation, Steve Hounsome
Practical Spirituality, Steve Hounsome

Psychic Self Defence - Real Solutions, Jan Brodie
Real Fairies, David Tame
Reality - How It Works & Why It Mostly Doesn't, Rik Dent
Romany Tapestry, Michael Houghton
Runic Astrology, Nigel Pennick
Sacred Animals, Gordon MacLellan
Sacred Celtic Animals, Marion Davies, Ill. Simon Rouse
Sacred Dorset - On the Path of the Dragon, Peter Knight
Sacred Grove - The Mysteries of the Forest, Yvonne Aburrow
Sacred Geometry, Nigel Pennick
Sacred Nature, Ancient Wisdom & Modern Meanings, A Cooper
Sacred Ring - Pagan Origins of British Folk Festivals, M. Howard
Season of Sorcery - On Becoming a Wisewoman, Poppy Palin
Seasonal Magic - Diary of a Village Witch, Paddy Slade
Secret Places of the Goddess, Philip Heselton
Secret Signs & Sigils, Nigel Pennick
The Secrets of East Anglian Magic, Nigel Pennick
A Seeker's Guide To Past Lives, Paul Williamson
Seeking Pagan Gods, Teresa Moorey
A Seer's Guide To Crystal Divination, Gale Halloran
Self Enlightenment, Mayan O'Brien
Soul Resurgence, Poppy Palin
Spirits of the Air, Jaq D Hawkins
Spirits of the Water, Jaq D Hawkins
Spirits of the Fire, Jaq D Hawkins
Spirits of the Aether, Jaq D Hawkins
Spirits of the Earth, Jaq D Hawkins
Stony Gaze, Investigating Celtic Heads John Billingsley
Stumbling Through the Undergrowth , Mark Kirwan-Heyhoe
Subterranean Kingdom, The, revised 2nd ed, Nigel Pennick
Symbols of Ancient Gods, Rhiannon Ryall
Talking to the Earth, Gordon MacLellan
Talking With Nature, Julie Hood
Taming the Wolf - Full Moon Meditations, Steve Hounsome
Teachings of the Wisewomen, Rhiannon Ryall
The Other Kingdoms Speak, Helena Hawley
Transformation of Housework, Ben Bushill
Treading the Mill - Practical CraftWorking in Modern Traditional Witchcraft by Nigel Pearson
Tree: Essence of Healing, Simon & Sue Lilly
Tree: Essence, Spirit & Teacher, Simon & Sue Lilly
Tree Seer, Simon & Sue Lilly
Torch and the Spear, Patrick Regan
Understanding Chaos Magic, Jaq D Hawkins
Understanding Second Sight, Dilys Gater
Understanding Spirit Guides, Dilys Gater

Understanding Star Children, Dilys Gater
The Urban Shaman, Dilys Gater
Vortex - The End of History, Mary Russell
Walking the Tides - Seasonal Rhythms and Traditional Lore in Natural Craft by Nigel Pearson
Warp and Weft - In Search of the I-Ching, William de Fancourt
Warriors at the Edge of Time, Jan Fry
Water Witches, Tony Steele
Way of the Magus, Michael Howard
Weaving a Web of Magic, Rhiannon Ryall
West Country Wicca, Rhiannon Ryall
What's Your Poison? vol 1, Tina Tarrant
Wheel of the Year, Teresa Moorey & Jane Brideson
Wildwitch - The Craft of the Natural Psychic, Poppy Palin
Wildwood King , Philip Kane
A Wisewoman's Book of Tea Leaf Reading, Pat Barki
The Witching Path, Moira Stirland
The Witch's Kitchen, Val Thomas
The Witches' Heart, Eileen Smith
Witches of Oz, Matthew & Julia Philips
Witchcraft Myth Magic Mystery and... Not Forgetting Fairies, Ralph Harvey
Wondrous Land - The Faery Faith of Ireland by Dr Kay Mullin
Working With Crystals, Shirley o'Donoghue
Working With Natural Energy, Shirley o'Donoghue
Working With the Merlin, Geoff Hughes
Your Talking Pet, Ann Walker
The Zodiac Experience, Patricia Crowther

FREE detailed catalogue
Contact: Capall Bann Publishing, Auton Farm, Milverton, Somerset, TA4 1NE
www.capallbann.co.uk